Ethereum for Architects and Developers

With Case Studies and Code Samples in Solidity

Debajani Mohanty

Apress®

Ethereum for Architects and Developers

Debajani Mohanty
Noida, Uttar Pradesh, India

ISBN-13 (pbk): 978-1-4842-4074-8   ISBN-13 (electronic): 978-1-4842-4075-5
https://doi.org/10.1007/978-1-4842-4075-5

Library of Congress Control Number: 2018961998

Copyright © 2018 by Debajani Mohanty

Managing Director, Apress Media LLC: Welmoed Spahr
Acquisitions Editor: Celestin Suresh John
Development Editor: Matthew Moodie
Coordinating Editor: Aditee Mirashi

Cover designed by eStudioCalamar

Cover image designed by Freepik (www.freepik.com)

Distributed to the book trade worldwide by Springer Science+Business Media New York, 233 Spring Street, 6th Floor, New York, NY 10013. Phone 1-800-SPRINGER, fax (201) 348-4505, e-mail orders-ny@springer-sbm.com, or visit www.springeronline.com. Apress Media, LLC is a California LLC and the sole member (owner) is Springer Science + Business Media Finance Inc (SSBM Finance Inc). SSBM Finance Inc is a Delaware corporation.

For information on translations, please e-mail rights@apress.com, or visit www.apress.com/rights-permissions.

Apress titles may be purchased in bulk for academic, corporate, or promotional use. eBook versions and licenses are also available for most titles. For more information, reference our Print and eBook Bulk Sales web page at www.apress.com/bulk-sales.

Any source code or other supplementary material referenced by the author in this book is available to readers on GitHub via the book's product page, located at www.apress.com/978-1-4842-4074-8. For more detailed information, please visit www.apress.com/source-code.

Printed on acid-free paper

This book is dedicated to my loving mother, Mrs. Nirupama Mohanty, who was recently diagnosed with breast cancer stage 1 and is undergoing treatment for complete recovery as I write this manuscript. We have been together during the most difficult phases in life, and this battle too we'll win.

Table of Contents

About the Author

Debajani Mohanty is a senior architect with NIIT Technologies Ltd in Delhi, NCR, and has almost 17 years of experience in the industry. She has been involved in large projects and has built many scalable enterprise B2B and B2C products in the travel, e-governance, e-commerce, and BFSI domains. Writing complex technical articles in easy-to-understand language is a forte that has earned her close to 10,000 followers on social media.

Debajani is the author of the bestseller *BlockChain: From Concept to Execution*, which has been translated to other languages such as German. Debajani is an honorary faculty member at Amity University Online. She is also a NASSCOM event speaker and on the international panels of mentors at Kerala Blockchain Academy, the first blockchain academy in India.

Debajani is also a woman activist and writer. She has been felicitated by Nobel Peace Prize winner Mr. Kailash Satyarthi for her outstanding contributions to women empowerment in the field of literature.

About the Technical Reviewer

Pon ArunKumar Ramalingam is an IT cognitive applications development consultant who has extensive experience in building full stack applications, using the Ethereum blockchain, implementing machine learning, and implementing enterprise resource planning suites of applications. He runs his own strategic sourcing and consulting company serving clients in the areas of human capital management, campus solutions, financials, and supply chain.

At ETHDenver, he won a hackathon on building decentralized Ethereum applications for societal cause, addressing the needs of street artists. He has worked for several fortune 500 companies and startups in North America and Asia Pacific. His career with Hexaware Technologies and Ford Motor Company brought him a lot of accolades for the services that he provided while relentlessly innovating ways to use emerging technology to solve real-world customer problems. His mastery in the emerging Ethereum blockchain and machine learning technologies has been showcased in various meetup presentations.

He is a wonderful team player, developer, and solution design architect and is a certified service-oriented architect professional. He has a BS in Engineering degree in computer science from the Sri Krishna College of Engineering and Technology at Bharathiar University in Coimbatore, Tamil Nadu, India. He currently lives in Concord, North Carolina.

Acknowledgments

This book is possible because of combined effort of many; my work is so small it causes only little ripples in a massive ocean. Thank you to the following people from all aspects of my life who have contributed to my success: my grandmother, Mrs. Renuka Pal Das; mother, Mrs. Nirupama Mohanty; father, Dr. N. K. Mohanty; uncle, Dr. N. R. Das; and husband, Dr. Rajul Rastogi, for always being there in times of need.

The woman-friendly workplace at NIIT Technologies Ltd has been a boon for me. Many thanks to our chairman Mr. Rajendra S. Pawar, vice chairman Mr. Arvind Thakur, CEO Mr. Sudhir Singh, senior vice president Mr. Suvrata Acharya, and my manager, Mr. Harish Nanda, for consistent motivation throughout my literary journey.

Preface

Since writing my first book on the blockchain technology, I have been invited to many discussions and have been approached by many startups to discuss how to initiate decentralized applications or products on either blockchain or distributed ledger technology.

Interestingly, most people I have met have little understanding of the capabilities and limitations of the blockchain technology. The hype has caused business leaders to spend time investigating use cases that are not necessarily good fits for a blockchain. Industry is still not sure how businesses can get benefits from this blockchain tsunami. To be precise, most blockchain experts today mint money from the market either by offering training programs or by working on initial coin offerings because business leaders are skeptical about blockchain technology and its potential and are still waiting for the right moment to go ahead with its implementation.

Unlike others, I am a late starter in the world of blockchains. In my first book, *BlockChain: From Concept to Execution*, I summarized most of the blockchain frameworks available on the market and where you can use them. However, as I took a deeper dive into the architecture and implementation details of these frameworks, I ran into a few roadblocks learning how to use them in real life, and I couldn't find much information available in books, via training programs, or on web sites. I expected to find a straightforward, comprehensive tutorial that covered all the basic necessities, such as verifying proofs and setting up tests, that would help a novice like me, but I came up empty-handed. As a result, I decided to write a book to help out others looking for the same details.

PREFACE

This book that I finally ended up writing is a perfect amalgamation of learning to use the blockchain technology at the same time as evaluating profitable, salable business use cases and their implementations using Ethereum, the most widely used blockchain framework in today's market. With step-by-step tutorials, examples, and pictorial representations and flowcharts, the book is suitable for even novices because of its easy readability. At the same time, it has many case studies with basic implementation details across verticals that will give architects and business leaders some vision of how and where this technology can be used to earn maximum profitability. Readers can use the sample code, enhance it per their respective business needs, and gradually develop and test decentralized applications before going to production.

Guidelines to Use the Book

Ethereum for Architects and Developers is an excellence book on Ethereum that explores the entire Ethereum ecosystem with step-by-step examples and plenty of theory, labs, and live use cases.

Ethereum today is the most widely used blockchain framework on the market; however, the main issues for learning Ethereum are the lack of trainers and its inadequate documentation. To learn Ethereum, developers, architects, and business leaders have to collect data from different web sites, blogs, articles, and YouTube videos. *Ethereum for Architects and Developers* should fill that vacuum by providing content suitable to all stakeholders consolidated in one place. On this reading journey, you will be introduced to blockchain concepts, decentralized applications, Ethereum architecture, Solidity smart contract programming with examples, and finally instructions on testing, debugging, and deploying smart contracts. Best practices to write contracts are explained in the most efficient way with ample examples to guide developers to write high-quality contracts. Later chapters will be most beneficial for business leaders and architects as the book will cover different business verticals such as finance, travel, supply chain, insurance, land registry, and more with flowcharts, diagrams, and sample code that stakeholders can refer to, enhance, and deploy in live projects.

GUIDELINES TO USE THE BOOK

The book will be useful for readers of every background who are eager to develop Ethereum decentralized applications, want to learn its architecture, or are interested in exploring different use cases that can be implemented using the Ethereum blockchain framework across business verticals. By the end of the book, readers will have enough information about how the optimal usage of Ethereum can create value for their business processes by eliminating middleman costs and bringing transparency to the creation of deduplicated, fraud-proof data storage for the smoother execution of business.

CHAPTER 1

The World of Blockchains

"I remember knowing, for a while, for a long time, that I was kind of abnormal in some sense."

—Vitalik Buterin

In my childhood my grandfather used to tell me stories of how to create an immense amount of wealth in a short time, of course in an honest way, and then more importantly how to keep it all safe. While most little girls my age were fascinated by fairytales, I found wealth creation ideas much more alluring and a means to be a powerful someone someday later in life. With time I came to know I was not the only one in this game. People of all ages think about this puzzle of "creation of wealth" and "securing it." Be it gold, spices, cattle, slaves, land, or oil, wealth has taken on different forms in the exchange of goods between parties and countries. Human history has witnessed many demonetizations where an existing currency is invalidated, followed by remonetization, in which a form of payment is restored as legal tender. Currencies were a mere representation of exchange media and yet carried no value without the backing of kings, emperors, or ruling governments. Cryptocurrency is one such currency; its distribution and exchange are entirely confined to the digital world. Bitcoin might not be the first digital currency, yet it's the first successful cryptocurrency on the market.

© Debajani Mohanty 2018
D. Mohanty, *Ethereum for Architects and Developers*,
https://doi.org/10.1007/978-1-4842-4075-5_1

Why Bitcoin Took the Market by Storm

In the last three to four decades many people have tried to work on digital or electronic currencies but have failed because of technical or regulatory issues. Even today companies such as PayPal, ECash, WebMoney, Liberty Reserve, Payoneer, and CashU use digitalized currency but through centralized systems. So, what was new about Bitcoin that made us all crazy?

These are some benefits:

- Low transaction fees

- Immunity to fraud

- Instantaneous settlements

- Prevention of identity theft

- Popularity

- Universally accepted (mostly)

Over the years, the price of Bitcoin has gone on a roller-coaster ride. While many countries such as the United States, Canada, Australia, and the European Union have gladly and openly embraced Bitcoin, there are a few that are still adverse to it. Sooner or later, I am hopeful in our lifetime a day will arrive when sectioned currencies will be entirely replaced by their digital counterparts.

The most beautiful part of Bitcoin, however, is its underlying mechanism to store data that is immutable, is immune to fraud, and uses cryptology in a secure way for sharing data across parties. This revolutionary new technology is called the *blockchain*. In other words, Bitcoin is a peer-to-peer electronic cash that is valuable over legacy systems because of the autonomous monetary benefits that it brings in a decentralized manner. The blockchain is the technology of storing records or data as blocks; it is similar to linked lists that use cryptographic hashing algorithms and Merkle trees.

In the last decade, investment in blockchains has risen exponentially. According to a research report published by MarketsandMarkets, the market is expected to grow from $623 million in 2018 to $15,455 million by 2023, at a compound annual growth rate (CAGR) of 90.1 percent during the forecast period.

Blockchains and Smart Contracts, the Need of the Hour

In a digital world, contracts have the potential to run the entire ecosystem. Let's just think about the role of contracts in our day-to-day lives.

In today's world, contracts define our economy and business, legal, and political systems. Be it purchasing a property, buying an asset, getting a job, buying insurance, or verifying your identity, contracts play a crucial role. Contracts are even established for interactions between political parties, nations, organizations, and individuals. Practically, processes take a massive amount of time when contracts are kind of slowed down in real life. At each stage, they need approval from authorities, and at each stage there could be obstructions due to the inefficiencies of individual, groups, businesses, or laws.

What if you could automate all these processes for a smooth execution?

This is where the beauty of the blockchain comes in. The blockchain that was invented by the mysterious Satoshi Nakamoto for the first cryptocurrency Bitcoin is capable of registering transactions in a secure way; in addition, with programmed smart contracts, it can trigger transactions automatically, as discussed in later sections of the book.

Maybe in a couple of years, with the help of blockchains, we can live in a completely automated digital world where contracts are embedded in code and stored in databases that are transparent, are shared, and are protected from deletion, tampering, and revision. Signatures would be digital and could be identified, validated, stored, and shared. This might lead to a cultural change where intermediaries such as lawyers, brokers, and bankers are longer be needed. Transactions and interactions between individuals, organizations, machines, and algorithms would be frictionless.

The blockchain has immense potential, and as per many it's the most significant invention since the Internet itself; per others, it's only hype. The barrier is not only in the technology that is still at its infancy but also with governance, organizational, cultural, and even societal issues. Many experts believe that we are years away from a world that's completely "blockchainified." The change might be slow but will definitely be steady. It will take years to transform our businesses, social systems, and governments. It's just like the initial credit card days when people used to feel safe staying away from ATMs and plastic, preferring the good old procedure of keeping cash in their wallets. So, it would be wrong in this book to jump to the code unless you understand blockchains in totality, the big-picture ecosystem, and the practical hindrances that you may face even if you are the best coder in the world.

The intent of this book is not only to train you in Ethereum programming; you will find many books and web sites for that. This book will explain the whole blockchain ecosystem and guide you with use cases and with code templates that you can use to build your proof of concepts (PoCs) and pilots in almost no time. By the end of the book and after some practice and analysis, you will have enough insight and ability not only to work on blockchain projects but also to advise your key stakeholders how to get the most out of this disruptive technology for your business.

Note   As quoted on its web site (`https://www.ethereum.org/`), Ethereum is a decentralized platform for applications that runs exactly as programmed without any chance of fraud, censorship, or third-party interference.

Introduction to Blockchains

Before going any further, here are few features to broadly define a blockchain:

- It is a distributed ledger or register. Some may call it a special type of database, but let's call it a register or ledger.

- It could be public or private.

- Every node in the network carries a copy of the ledger.

- There is no single point of failure and no downtime.

- Data in a blockchain is immutable; in other words, once the data is stored, it can't be altered.

- Each record in the database is known as a *block* that points to the previous block in the chain.

- Each new block consists of a group of transactions that is added to the end of the blockchain.

Please revisit this section after you learn more about blockchains in later sections where they're more thoroughly explained.

Business Problem

Before learning about Ethereum in detail, you may wonder why the market is so fascinated with blockchains. If a blockchain is a storing mechanism, you know that many such mechanisms exist in industry and have for decades.

The answer is that the blockchain is not useful for storing data for an individual but is useful for multiple parties, especially who do not trust each other and yet want to share data for some business transaction.

So, let's find out the different mechanisms used in the current market by enterprises such as banks, financial organizations, global distribution systems (GDSs) in travel, or supply-chain systems to communicate with each other. Consider that three independent organizations are trying to do some business together in any vertical. Before their collaboration, they had their individual data in their respective silos. Now that they come together, what are the possible ways to share data?

Fully Distributed Model

Most current projects must be aligned with the model specified in Figure 1-1 where each of the three organizations maintain their own data and communicate through some web service or messaging protocol. There could be many problems in such a process.

- Most of the data would be redundant, with each organization carrying their own version.

- Data across organizations might not be in sync because of latency issues.

- Processes would be wasteful; reconciliations would be complex and expensive.

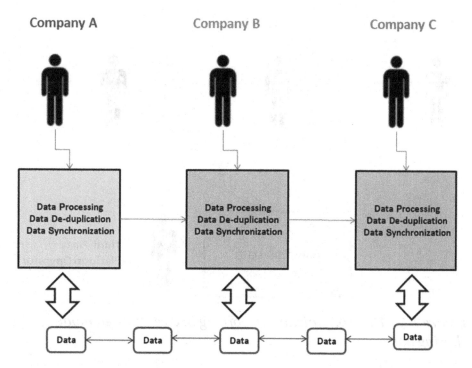

Figure 1-1. *Three organizations working in a distributed mode of sharing data*

Fully Centralized Model

You have already seen an issue with distributed systems, so now how can you move to a completely shared model that would be secure and neutral to all these organizations? As shown in Figure 1-2, mostly organizations achieve this by delegating this responsibility to a third party that works as a common platform for all parties to store and share data.

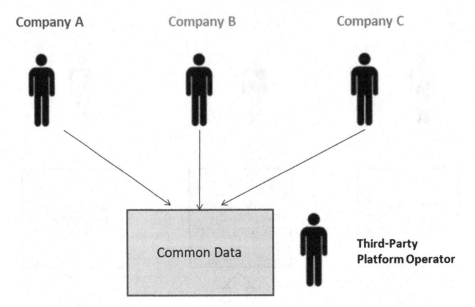

Figure 1-2. *Three organizations working in a centralized mode of sharing data*

Let's explore the issues here.

- This is an expensive way because third parties will charge for such a service.

- The third party may have a conflict of interest with an individual organization. A particular party may not agree with the data for some reason.

- There could be legal issues leading to data regulation.

So, what could be the model where parties can share data in the most efficient way so that

- Data is in sync across all the networks

- Redundancy is at a minimum or nonexistent

- Expenses due to reconciliations are less frequent

- Auditing is easy

The new mechanism that comes to mind is a distributed ledger technology (DLT).

DLT, or the Decentralized Peer-to-Peer Model

Distributed ledger technology, as shown in Figure 1-3, is a mechanism that works in a peer-to-peer fashion, which is different from each of the two previous models. Using DLT, you can develop applications and platforms where ownership is shared across the network of collaborating companies, completely eliminating the need for a third party to operate the applications on your behalf.

- Mutual processes and data are shared as tamper-proof single sources of truth that entirely remove the need for traditional integration, data translation, duplication, and redundancy.

- Data synchronization and consensus are provided by the DLT platform. Applications are built once, in collaboration, and used by many parties.

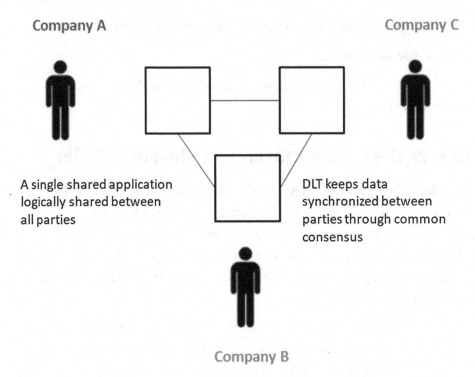

Company A

A single shared application logically shared between all parties

Company C

DLT keeps data synchronized between parties through common consensus

Company B

Figure 1-3. *Three organizations working in a peer-to-peer mode of sharing data*

Now that you broadly know all three models, let's see how nodes representing parties can be pictorially represented. Figure 1-4 compares the centralized client-server and peer-to-peer models.

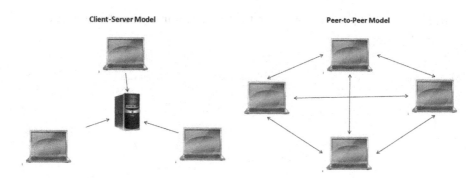

Figure 1-4. *Client-server versus peer-to-peer models*

Now let's see how these two patterns can be further modified by bringing a higher intensity of decentralization to the overall network (see Figure 1-5).

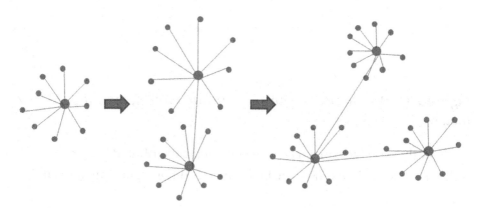

Figure 1-5. *Client-server model in more and more decentralized mode*

In Figure 1-6, observe how peer-to-peer networks work when there is no central server.

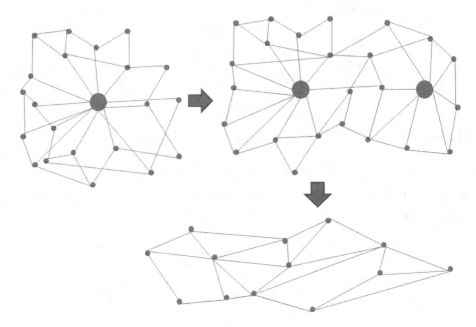

Figure 1-6. *Peer-to-peer model in more and more decentralized mode*

Now that you are convinced why you need a distributed ledger technology, let's discuss how the blockchain is different or similar to DLT.

DLT vs. Blockchains

The blockchain is a special use case of distributed ledger technology. This is how they are the same:

- Both use public/private key cryptography.

- Both use hashing.

- Both use a peer-to-peer model for communication.

This is how they are different:

- The blockchain uses native currency, which is a mandate. DLT does not.

- The blockchain is distributed; in other words, all data can be visible to all nodes. DLT is not.

- The blockchain is permission-less. DLT is not.

- The blockchain works with proof of work (though soon Ethereum is coming up with proof of stake). DLT does not.

Benefits of Blockchains

You may wonder whether the blockchain is another type of database and why it was created in the first place. Please note that the blockchain was introduced through Bitcoin, a cryptocurrency, and it was conceptualized to address the need of digital currency that a traditional database cannot.

- The data in a blockchain ledger can't be altered.

- It's a highly secured database that uses public and private keys for transactions.

- The database is publicly available for everyone to validate and add transactions.

- Since the blockchain is decentralized, there is no downtime in the blockchain, and hence transactions can be added at any time and from anywhere.

- It could be public or private as per the needs of an individual or business and is hence flexible.

- The ledger is open to auditing anytime.

Blockchain Transactions and Blocks

Now let's see how data is added to a blockchain ledger. Consider a book as represented in Figure 1-7 that has 100 pages with a page number embossed at the top of each page. If one page is torn out from the book, the reader could easily figure it out. The same is true for a blockchain store.

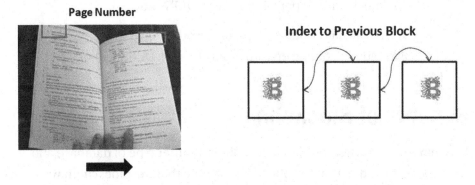

Figure 1-7. *Indexing in the blockchain*

As the name suggests, the blockchain is a chain of blocks where each block points to a previous block.

Each block consists of the following:

- A block header

- One or more transactions in the block

- An optional list of ommers, or uncle, blocks

- An optional fork here and there

If you compare a blockchain data store to a book, then each block represents a page in the book, and transactions quoted in the individual block are synonymous to lines on a page in the book.

The first block in a blockchain ledger, as shown in Figure 1-8, is known as a Genesis block. Ommers, or uncle, blocks are the detached blocks not chosen for inclusion in the consensus blockchain. However, miners (explained later in the chapter) still find a smaller number of tokens by discovering them.

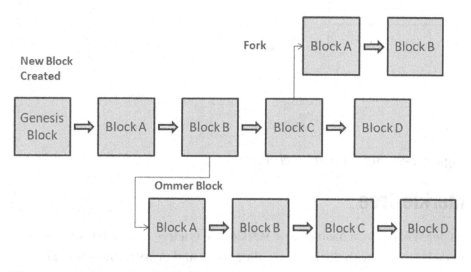

Figure 1-8. *How the blockchain progresses*

Block Header

A blockchain consists of a series of blocks that are joined together with special logic. Every block has a block header that has the following information, also shown in Figure 1-9:

- Hash of the previous block

- Timestamp

- Mining or difficulty level

- A proof-of-work nonce

- A root hash for the Merkle tree containing the transactions for that block

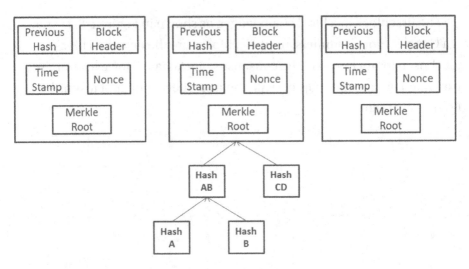

Figure 1-9. *Blocks in a blockchain*

Merkle Tree

As per Wikipedia, a hash tree or Merkle tree is a tree in which every leaf node is labeled with the hash of a data block and every nonleaf node is labeled with the cryptographic hash of the labels of its child nodes.

What does that mean? Well, a Merkle tree represents data in its nascent form as well as in its hashed value (see Figure 1-10). At the bottom of the tree you can see real values, which are called *leaf nodes*.

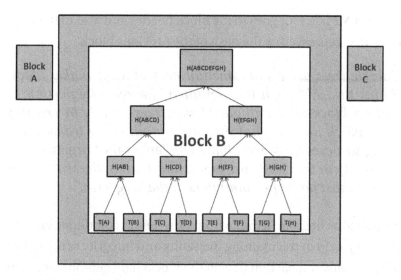

Figure 1-10. *Merkle tree*

Let's say in the following blockchain we have three blocks. In the middle block, B, there are eight transactions, from T(A) to T(H). Now let's see how the Merkle tree is formed.

1. Each of these transactions is first converted to their hash values, in other words, H(A) to H(H).

2. Each hash value is paired with another hash value next to it to create a new hash value, in other words, H(A) + H(B) = H(AB). What if you have an odd number of transactions, in other words, H(G) as the last hash? Then it creates a hash with itself, in other words, H(GG).

3. This process continues until you reach a single hash of all the transactions of the current block, in other words, H(ABCDEFGH). This is called the *Merkle root.*

Now this Merkle root goes to the block header and also to the next block where it gets saved as the hash of the previous block.

> *"Merkle trees are a fundamental part of what makes block-chains tick. Although it is definitely theoretically possible to make a blockchain without Merkle trees, simply by creating giant block headers that directly contain every transaction, doing so poses large scalability challenges that arguably put the ability to trustlessly use blockchains out of the reach of all but the most powerful computers in the long term."*

The previous lines are a quote from Ethereum's cofounder Vitalik Buterin. They help in maintaining the sanity and integrity of the entire blockchain. If any transaction data in the blockchain gets altered, then the hash value would be altered, and ultimately the Merkle root would be altered and would mismatch with the original Merkle root saved in the next block; hence, the blockchain would be invalidated. This is the magic formula with which data remains tamperproof and secure online in a public blockchain such as Bitcoin or Ethereum.

Double Spending

Double spending is an issue in a blockchain ecosystem, and different blockchain and DLT networks handle it using different algorithms. Let's say Party A has $100 and has to pay $100 to Party B and $100 to Party C. In the real world, this is not possible because the payment would be in physical currency. But in the digital world, especially in the blockchain ecosystem, if party A in quick succession creates two transactions to Party B and Party C each with $100 before the earlier one is confirmed, then it's possible that both transactions would be executed independently. This issue is called *double spending* (see Figure 1-11). Ethers shown in the picture are a type of crypto currency to be discussed later in the book.

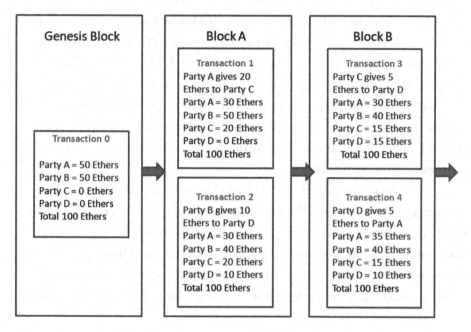

Figure 1-11. *Tracking transactions in a blockchain*

In a blockchain network, such issues are prevented by tracing each transaction closely. When the Genesis block is added, the network is assigned a finite supply of cryptocurrency, and then those currencies are exchanged between parties as the transactions go on. Each time a block is added, miners thoroughly calculate whether the entire supply remains the same, and no data is tampered with. Thus, double spending is completely avoided.

Blockchain Hashing

Hashing is an algorithm that takes any string as input and gives you another string as output that has a fixed length. It's nearly impossible to decipher the input from the output string. Also, it does not matter how many times or at whatever time interval you hash the input string; the output string will always remain the same. Also, the length of the output string will always remain the same for inputs big or small; only the output contents will be different. There are different industry-standard hashing algorithms available on the market such as SHA-1, SHA-2, SHA-256, and so on. Hashing is frequently used for comparing secure data; for example, passwords are most often never stored in databases in nascent form. Rather, their hashed value is stored, and whenever the user logs in again, the hash value of the supplied password is cross-checked with the saved hash value to authenticate the user.

So, why is hashing needed in a blockchain? As already discussed, in blockchains, you calculate the hash values of data and then create a hash of all the hashes of transactions and store it in the header of each block. Also, each block has a similar hash value as the previous block. This binds the entire blockchain together with complex logic. Hence, it is extremely difficult for any attacker to decipher the whole dataset with maligned data.

Public and Private Keys

When someone sends you cryptocoins over the blockchain, they actually send them to a hashed version of what's known as the *public key*. There is another key that is hidden from them, which is known as the *private key*. This private key is used to derive the public key. Everyone in the blockchain network knows their own private key. It's like a master key to your safe deposit box in a bank and should not be shared with anyone, unless you want your cryptocurrencies to be stolen (see Figure 1-12)!

Figure 1-12. Public and private keys

The private key is used to mathematically derive the public key, which is then transformed with a hash function to produce the address that other people can see. You receive cryptocurrencies that others send to your address.

At this point, you may be asking yourself, if a public key is derived from a private key, couldn't someone create a reverse key generator that derives the private keys from the public keys, allowing them to steal anyone's coins in the process? Cryptocurrencies solve this issue by using a complicated mathematical algorithm to generate the public keys: the algorithm makes it easy to generate public keys from private keys, but it is difficult to "reverse" the algorithm to accomplish the opposite (see Figure 1-13).

Figure 1-13. *The private key cannot be extracted from the public key*

Consensus

You already know the blockchain is a decentralized database where data is saved with a common consensus between all the parties. Consensus is never an issue with a traditional centralized database because it has a leader or a central authority responsible for making all the decisions, validating the data, and storing it. However, the blockchain is a public ledger that deals with multiple peers. So, how can all the participants agree on the current state of the blockchain and reach a common consensus to store data when they do not trust each other? Different blockchain and DLT frameworks have worked on this puzzle and have come up with different solutions. Broadly, the consensus mechanisms can be mainly divided into the following types:

- Proof of work (POW)

- Proof of stake (POS)

- Delegated proof of stake (DPOS)

- Proof of authority (POA)

- Practical Byzantine fault tolerance (PBFT)

- Directed acyclic graphs (DAGs)

Currently these consensus mechanisms have been widely adopted by different blockchain and DLT frameworks. A particular model can be chosen over others as per an organization's business demands. Performance, scalability, and security are major factors before picking any one of them over others.

Proof of Work

The proof of work was the first consensus mechanism introduced with Bitcoin. In POW, all the miners (mining is discussed later in the chapter) compete to solve a mathematical problem, and the one who solves it fastest becomes the winner. Soon other miners start validating it until it reaches an agreed-on percentage (51 percent or 90 percent as per the configuration). POW works on the "longest chain" rule; in other words, if there are forks created because of different miners agreeing to different side chains, then the longest chain that moves the fastest is the most trustworthy; soon others will start following that chain, and other side chains will be discarded.

Used by: Bitcoin, Ethereum

Advantages: Time tested, safe

Disadvantages: Too slow, massive power consumption

MINING

The process of validating transactions and adding a block to the blockchain framework is called *mining*. The participant users who mine are called *miners*. But why would someone like to be a miner? It's because the miners are rewarded with a fraction of cryptocurrency that fuels the blockchain framework.

Proof of Stake

POS consensus has nothing to do with mining, yet it still validates the blocks and adds to the blockchain. This collateral-based consensus algorithm depends on the validator's economic stake in the network. In other words, each validator must own some stake in the network by depositing some money into the network. In POS-based consensus for public blockchains, several validators take turns proposing and voting on the next block, and the weight of each validator's vote depends on the size of its deposit.

Used by: Ethereum's upcoming Casper model of consensus

Advantages: Security, reduced risk of centralization, and energy efficiency

Disadvantages: more prone to attack as there is no computational factor like with POW to keep the network safe

MINTING

In POS the entire process of validating a new block and getting a fraction of the cryptocurrency as a reward is called *minting* (not mining).

Delegated Proof of Stake

The DPOS is a variation of the POS consensus model where all the users vote to select the ones who will be the final approvers of transactions in a democratic way.

Used by: EOS, Bitshares

Advantages: Super-fast, scalable, and high energy efficiency

Disadvantages: None

Proof of Authority

POA is a modified version of POS where identity is at stake instead of monetary value. In this consensus model, transactions and blocks are validated by approved accounts, known as *validators*. Individuals get the right to be an approving authority only after producing their valid identity proof. Hence, there is no need for mining.

Used by: Ethereum's Parity

Advantages: Security, no mining, high in scalability and performance

Disadvantages: None

Practical Byzantine Fault Tolerance

The PBFT model of consensus is derived from the classic problem of wars in ancient times. Let's say several Byzantine generals with their respective groups of armies have surrounded an enemy fort. To conquer the fort, it's crucial that most of the generals attack the fort at the same time and work in unity. However, whether they will attack the fort and at what time is a collective decision between them all, which they would know by sharing data between each other. Let's say General 1 sends a message to Generals 2, 3, and 4 to attack at 4:30 p.m., and all send their acknowledgment to the proposal as "yes." However, it's possible that one of them is a traitor and will actually not oblige when a common attack is required. Consensus in such a system, which is equivalent to a win in the war, is achieved if a minimum particular threshold is achieved, in other words, two-thirds of all generals actually being loyal and working in unison.

Used by: Hyperledger, Ripple, Stellar

Advantages: High transaction throughput

Disadvantages: Centralized/permissioned

Directed Acyclic Graphs

DAGs are another type of consensus that comes with a data structure very different from the Blockchains and is far faster as well. Tangle is the DAG consensus algorithm used by IOTA. To send an IOTA transaction, you need to validate two previous transactions you've received.

Used by: IOTA, Hashgraph, Nano

Advantages: Infinitely scalable, speed increases as network grows, best suited for microtransactions

Disadvantages: Works well only with a large amount of traffic; without traffic may have initiation problem

Forks in Blockchains

If you start working with a blockchain framework such as Ethereum, often you will come across forks (see Figure 1-14). Forks in a blockchain are of two types.

- Soft fork

- Hard fork

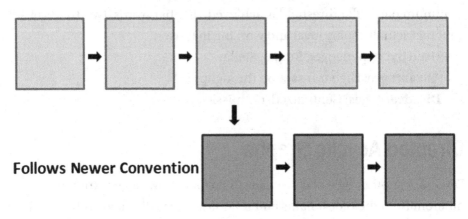

Figure 1-14. *A fork in the blockchain*

Soft Fork

While transactions are added to a block and the block gets validated by any consensus model such as POW or POA, a temporary fork might get created either accidentally or otherwise because people may have different versions of the same blockchain ledger. In most cases, the forks are sorted out as soon as most people on the network start accepting the longest chain as the moment of truth. The side chains are discarded and acknowledged as faulty blocks. They are called *soft forks*.

Soft forks have vulnerability for being exposed to denial-of-service (DoS) attacks that may prevent the network from processing valid transactions at negligible expense to the attacker. Just like any other DoS attacks, an attacker can flood the network with transactions that have high complexity for computation and end by performing an operation on the decentralized autonomous organization (DAO, to be explained later in book) contract. Therefore, you have to be careful with soft forks.

Hard Fork

Hard forks are needed from time to time as software has to pass through changes or version upgrades. In such processes, two different versions of the blockchain are created sharing the same origin, which is often called a *hard fork*. Depending upon this rule that denotes an intensity of change from the original version, the fork is labeled as a soft fork or hard fork. The primary difference between a soft fork and a hard fork is that soft forks are backward compatible whereas hard forks are not.

Bitcoin, whose Genesis or first block was created back in 2009, has undergone many hard forks since then, named as follows:

- Bitcoin XT

- Bitcoin Classic

- Bitcoin Unlimited

- Segregated Witness

- Bitcoin Cash

- Bitcoin Gold

- SegWit2X

Forks in Ethereum

Similarly, Ethereum has two forks so far, known as Ethereum and Ethereum Classic (see Figure 1-15).

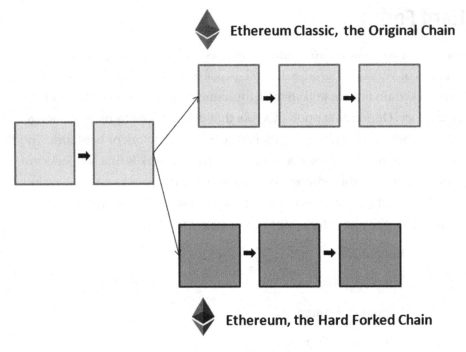

Figure 1-15. Forks in the Ethereum blockchain

While Classic is a hard fork that retains some of the original flavors of the Ethereum blockchain, it's not backward compatible, whereas the latter is a soft fork and gets all the benefits of being upgraded to all the latest improvements.

Types of Visibilities in Blockchain Networks

Blockchain networks have different visibilities (public, private, permissioned, consortium) that suit different business needs.

Public Blockchains

A blockchain is completely transparent and publicly accessible (through most likely the Internet), and transactions are open to all on the network. Public blockchains need volunteers or miners to validate and secure entries, through either POW, POS, or any other consensus method. Bitcoin is a perfect example of a public blockchain network. Even Ethereum in its nascent form is a public blockchain framework.

The advantages are that there are no infrastructure costs and there is no need to maintain servers or system administrators, which radically reduces the costs of creating and running decentralized applications.

Private Blockchains

In a private blockchain, all permissions are kept centralized with an organization.

A private blockchain is not decentralized; it's rather just a distributed database. It allows some organizations that have compliance and privacy requirements to implement a blockchain.

Monax and MultiChain are fine examples of private blockchains. Ethereum can be configured to work on a private blockchain network. In fact, many people nowadays prefer private blockchains because they do not want to expose their data to the entire world through a public network.

The advantages are that it scales well, has faster execution, and no token is needed to procure for mining.

Consortium or Federated Blockchains

A consortium blockchain is partly private. Instead of allowing any person with an Internet connection to participate in the verification of transactions or allowing only one company to have full control, a few selected nodes are predetermined. For example, in the case of international trade, the consortium may consist of participating banks, importers, exporters, ports of sending and receiving countries, custom officials, and so on. Some of these participants will have write access, and some or all will have read access.

A consortium blockchain is not fully decentralized like a public blockchain.

Quorum, R3 Corda, Hyperledger Fabric, and so on, are based on this principle. Like a private blockchain, they are fast, efficient, and secure.

Be it a fully decentralized public blockchain or a fully private blockchain or even a consortium blockchain, all have potential use cases, and there could be a blockchain solution that is a permutation of more than one of these. You have to study your business use case well and choose the right one that suits it the best.

Advantages of Ethereum

Since Ethereum debuted, many other blockchains as well as DLT frameworks have flooded the market; I included a few in "Leading Blockchain and DLT Protocols" section. However, Ethereum is still a blockchain haven for many. Here are a few reasons:

- Ethereum has been on the market since July 2015; it's the oldest player here.

- You can find a huge development network with Ethereum.

- There are plenty of tools and frameworks built on top of Ethereum such as Quorum, Truffle, MetaMask, and Embark.

- There are enough developers available with Ethereum skill sets.

- Most major cloud enablers as Amazon Web Service, Azure, Google Cloud, and so on, either have started providing Ethereum templates as part of the service or are planning to do so.

- Ethereum is open source.

Limitations of Ethereum

Though there are no disadvantages of Ethereum yet, being a public blockchain, it comes with a certain number of limitations.

- Public blockchains are not suitable for all.

- At the time of writing, Ethereum is slow. It takes 12 seconds for miners to validate and add a block to an Ethereum blockchain network. Perhaps with sharding this will improve. (We will discuss sharding in Chapter 10.)

A lot of extra work is needed to set up a private, permissioned network. Ethereum is not first choice here; use DLT instead for this. You will find quite a few DLTs available on the market; I have discussed a few briefly.

Leading Blockchain and DLT Protocols

Many blockchain and DLT frameworks are available on the market today. Let's discuss some of the most popular ones. If you want to know more, you may refer to my other book, *BlockChain: From Concept to Execution*, where I have detailed most of them.

Quorum

Quorum is the enterprise-focused version of Ethereum. Quorum addresses specific challenges to blockchain technology adoption within the financial industry and beyond. Quorum has developed capabilities to address the requirements of many industries and verticals.

Ripple

Ripple claims it's the "world's only enterprise blockchain solution for global payments." Unlike many other cryptocurrencies, Ripple is centralized and comes with a finite supply of currencies. Also, it claims to be the most scalable blockchain solution on the market.

Hyperledger Fabric

Hyperledger Fabric is one of the many projects running under the Hyperledger umbrella. Originally contributed by IBM, today it is the most widely used private permissioned framework on the market. While Ethereum has been running in production for the past few years, Hyperledger Fabric is still maturing. The July 2017 version claims to be production ready. In many ways, the architecture and features of Hyperledger Fabric are pretty similar to R3 Corda, as they are built on the same specification.

R3 Corda

R3 (R3CEV LLC) is a distributed database technology company that leads a consortium of more than 200 of the world's biggest banks and financial institutions in the research and development of blockchain database usage in the financial system.

R3 Corda is a joint venture that started in September 2015 between R3 and numerous banks and financial groups to create a framework that is more than a traditional blockchain. Corda is especially crafted to suit the needs of financial institutes with features such as speed, privacy, scalability, security, and so on.

MultiChain

MultiChain is another promising private permissioned blockchain framework made up of the Bitcoin fork. It's open source, it's well documented, and it comes with a low learning curve and fast deployment.

Symbiont

Founded in 2015, Symbiont is a blockchain technology company based in New York City, developing products in smart contracts and distributed ledgers for use in capital markets.

OpenChain

OpenChain is an open source, enterprise-ready blockchain technology platform most suitable to organizations wanting to issue and manage digital assets in a robust, secure, and scalable way.

Cardano

Launched in September 2017 by IOHK, Cardano is a decentralized blockchain platform on open source smart contracts that works on a proof-of-stake algorithm and provides a base for the cryptocurrency ADA. Its first version was released in September 2017.

IOTA

IOTA is a distributed ledger protocol just like Ethereum, yet it comes with a revolutionary new architecture called Tangle. With fee-less micropayments, it will enable communication between connected devices and, per IOTA, will lead to a novel machine economy for the backbone of the Internet of Things.

EOS

Based on a white paper published in 2017, EOS is another player in the open source blockchain market. It's a blockchain-based, decentralized operating system, designed to support commercial-scale decentralized applications by providing all the necessary core functionality including databases, accounts with permissions, scheduling, authentication, and communication between the application and the Internet, thus allowing developers to focus on their own particular business logic. Loaded with features, it's often termed the "Ethereum killer" or "Ethereum with a motor."

Hashgraph

The Hedera hashgraph platform is less constrained than a blockchain and provides a new form of distributed consensus. It caters to the same group of people who don't know or trust each other to securely collaborate and transact online without the need for a trusted intermediary. The advantages of this platform over a blockchain are that it's lightning fast, secure, and fair, and it doesn't require compute-intensive proof of work. As per some experts, Hedera hashgraph is pretty much likely to replace blockchains altogether.

Most Ambitious Ethereum Projects in Production

In the blockchain race, Ethereum has left everyone behind by being in production well ahead of others. Though most of the Ethereum projects running in production are initial coin offerings (ICOs), let's discuss a few non-ICO projects that are considered leading works in this space. Once you are done with the book, please revisit this section and the web sites related to each of them. These organizations are mostly startups that have used Ethereum to give shape to their imagination and have created leading decentralized applications using Ethereum.

- *uPort*: This is a digital identity platform recently launched in Zug, a city in Switzerland where the city government can issue a Zug ID to its citizens, which is a digital verification of their citizenship.

- *Rentberry*: Rentberry is the first rental platform that aims to solve all the major issues found in renting property today. Powered by a blockchain, Rentberry certainly is a fascinating concept on offer that has prompted even Forbes to pick Rentberry as one of its top ten real estate startups for 2018.

- *Coinlancer*: Coinlancer is a decentralized job market built on the Ethereum platform that empowers burgeoning freelancers and clients from across the globe.

- *Status*: Status is an Ethereum light client targeting Android and iOS that gives users options to browse, chat, and make payments securely on the decentralized Web.

- *FairWin*: This is a decentralized gaming technology platform based on Ethereum that brings innovation to gambling games.

- *EtherSport*: EtherSport is a platform where people all over the world can place bets on sporting events. The lottery mechanism is done through Ethereum contracts.

- *Tap Coin*: Ethereum-based Tap Coin is a utility token that allows gamers to convert their in-game earned and premium currencies to Tap Coin.

- *ChoonHQ*: This is a music ecosystem based on the Ethereum network that provides a music streaming service and digital payments ecosystem designed to solve some of the music industry's most fundamental problems.

- *Etheal*: This is healthcare based on the Ethereum blockchain that brings transparency to the $100 billion medical tourism industry and already has 2.5 million visits per year.

- *Mavin*: This is a rewards-based blockchain platform for marketing influencers.

CHAPTER 2

Ethereum Architecture

"The thing that I often ask startups on top of Ethereum is, 'Can you please tell me why using the Ethereum blockchain is better than using Excel?' And if they can come up with a good answer, that's when you know you've got something really interesting."

—Vitalik Buterin

According to *Forbes*, "Ethereum is the first generic blockchain platform that allows users to easily create and deploy their decentralized and trustless applications. It has created incredible opportunities in the fintech space." This chapter will introduce you to the entire ecosystem of Ethereum. Later chapters will discuss its specific components in more detail.

Bitcoin vs. Ethereum

Ethereum was introduced in 2015 as a hard fork from Bitcoin. It's the second cryptocurrency invented by Russian-Canadian programmer and writer as well as teenage prodigy Vitalik Buterin. Vitalik, who earlier worked on Bitcoin, was not satisfied with the mechanism that Bitcoin worked with and came up with his improved version of the blockchain framework called Ethereum.

© Debajani Mohanty 2018
D. Mohanty, *Ethereum for Architects and Developers*,
https://doi.org/10.1007/978-1-4842-4075-5_2

Comparing Bitcoin and Ethereum is like comparing apples and oranges. In fact, Bitcoin and Ethereum were introduced to the market with different purposes. The sole purpose of Bitcoin was to create an alternate digital currency in the market and thus create a payment and transaction system that is completely safe and transparent. By contrast, Ethereum was developed as a platform that facilitates peer-to-peer contracts and applications via its own native currency called *ether*. The primary purpose of ether is to facilitate and monetize the working of Ethereum to enable developers to build and run distributed applications (called *Dapps*).

Ethereum also introduced a revolutionary new concept called a *smart contract*, which is a "Turing complete" language.

Turing Complete

A Turing machine is a theoretical mathematical machine or model of computation invented by Alan Turing in 1936 that defines an abstract machine that manipulates symbols on a strip of tape according to a table of rules. It's simple yet can simulate any computer algorithm, no matter how complicated. It's widely believed that Turing's theory later gave foundation to computer science.

A machine or computer or language is considered "Turing complete" if it can solve any problem that a Turing machine can be given an appropriate algorithm and the necessary time and memory.

Ethereum Virtual Machine

Ethereum is a Turing complete blockchain framework, as it gives a foundation to programming languages using which you can write contracts that can solve any reasonable computational problem. Ethereum is controlled by the Ethereum Virtual Machine (EVM), a consensus-based virtual machine that decodes the compiled contracts in bytecodes and executes them on the Ethereum network nodes. It also uses algorithms to prevent denial-of-service attacks that are widely observed in cryptocurrency markets.

As shown in Figure 2-1, the Ethereum blockchain network is a group of EVMs, or *nodes*, connected to every other node in a peer-to-peer mechanism. Each node consists of a copy of the entire blockchain data store and competes with other nodes to mine the next block by validating transactions. If a new block is added, the blockchain gets updated and is propagated to the entire network so that every node is in sync.

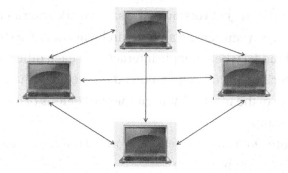

Figure 2-1. *Peer-to-peer model*

Consensus Mechanism

Ethereum currently uses the same proof-of-work (POW) model for mining as Bitcoin. However, soon it has plans to switch to a proof-of-stake mechanism called Casper, whose first version will be available in 2018. Also, the current POW model of Ethereum is much more efficient than that of Bitcoin for which usually a block is added to the network every 12 seconds.

Decentralized Autonomous Organization

In a traditional organization, people work in a hierarchical fashion to achieve a common goal. Each stakeholder in such a situation has a clearly defined scope of work that is aligned to the policies, rules, and regulations of the organization written on paper and approved by law.

As per the wiki page `https://en.wikipedia.org/wiki/Decentralized_autonomous_organization`, "A decentralized autonomous organization (DAO), sometimes labeled a decentralized autonomous corporation (DAC), is an organization that is run through rules encoded as computer programs called smart contracts. A DAO's financial transaction record and program rules are maintained on a blockchain."

A DAO is just the digital version of the same work described earlier. However, instead of a centralized and hierarchical system, a DAO follows a decentralized model where people interact with each other according to a protocol specified in code and enforced on the blockchain. Smart contracts are one of the most complex implementations of this model that we will discuss soon.

The Ethereum DAO crowd sale is now one of the most successful crowd-funding campaigns to date.

Smart Contracts

Smart contracts are an important part of a blockchain framework. Using them, people can trade on the Internet without the need of a middleman. They are governed by neither central authorities nor human intervention.

Smart contracts are self-executing contracts with the terms of the contract between the buyer and seller directly written into lines of code. Smart contracts permit trusted transactions and agreements to be carried out among disparate, anonymous parties without the need for a central authority, legal system, or external enforcement mechanism. They render transactions traceable, transparent, and irreversible.

In Ethereum there are three languages available to write smart contracts.

1. Solidity

2. Vyper

3. LLL

We'll discuss only Solidity here.

Solidity

Solidity is the official and most widely used language in the Ethereum network; using it, smart contracts are written that are agreed on between two parties. It may seem like JavaScript, but actually it's more like Java for its statically typed feature. These contracts can be validated using Remix (`https://remix.ethereum.org/`), a browser-based IDE with an integrated compiler. Solidity comes with its own compiler that generates machine-level bytecode that can run on the EVM.

Gas

Gas is the fuel that powers an Ethereum network. In a public Ethereum blockchain network, to lure more and more miners to work on validating the transaction, the transaction creator assigns a particular amount of gas to the transaction, which has to be paid to the miner who mines the transaction the fastest.

Gas comes with the following keywords you must remember while programming:

- *Gas limit*: This is the maximum amount of gas you are willing to pay to the miner for validating the transaction. The higher the price, the greater the

chance that your transaction will be executed faster
as that will attract more miners to prioritize your
transaction over others. Also, insufficient gas in the gas
limit will result in a failed transaction.

- *Gas price*: This is the amount of ether or fraction of
  ether you are willing to spend on every unit of gas. The
  gas price is usually some amount of gwei, which is a
  fraction of a wei. Wei is the smallest unit of ether, and
  gwei is equivalent to 1000000000 wei.

- *Gas cost*: This is a static value for a particular operation.
  Figure 2-2 shows you the cost associated with different
  operations.

Now that you know all the terminology, are you eager to find out the
direct conversion rate between ether and gas? You can check `https://
walletinvestor.com/converter/ethereum/gas/`. In Figure 2-2 the
exchange price is shown as of July 2018.

1 Ethereum = 46.375410 Gas (GAS)

Date (today): 26. July 2018 04:47 PM (GMT)

Name	Price USD	Market Cap USD	Available Supply	Volume 24h USD	% 24h	Price Graph (7d)
Ethereum	474.896	47,969,102,198	100,934,000	1,581,923,513	⌃ 1.09	
Gas	10.246	103,857,362	10,128,400	3,534,650	⌄ -2.17	

Figure 2-2. *Ether to gas conversion*

Refer to the Ethereum yellow pages at `https://ethereum.github.io/
yellowpaper/paper.pdf` to get the gas and cost details.

While executing a public Ethereum blockchain, architects
and developers should be extremely careful to follow the correct
architectural pattern and guidelines for functions, variables, and so on,

before starting to develop a Dapp project. Refer to the conversion chart throughout the development cycle. Learning Solidity programming to run on a public Ethereum blockchain could be relatively easy, but more importantly a developer needs to know how to write the code to use the gas prices optimally to get maximum efficiency for executing smart contracts. This will be covered in Chapter 6 where I discuss best practices for Solidity programming.

Where Does Data Get Stored in Ethereum?

Ethereum is used to build decentralized applications using smart contracts, which I will cover in detail in next chapters. A contract is a combination of data (such as state variables) and functions to store that data to a specific address on the Ethereum blockchain. At a later point of time and as needed, data can be retrieved and used further.

Ethereum holds a set of accounts. Every account has an owner and a balance, which is some ether.

If I prove my identity, I can transfer ether (which is the cryptocurrency, or money in another form) from my account to another. This is an atomic operation called a *transaction*.

Ethereum Accounts

As mentioned, every account has an owner and a balance. But some of these accounts are special; they own themselves. At creation time, we give them a piece of code and memory. That's a smart contract.

A smart contract is like a smart bank account that executes some code when it receives transactions. This transaction happens within the blockchain, which is public, replicated, and validated by the network. A smart contract has a balance, some code, and some storage that is persistent. Also, a smart contract won't fail because of a power outage in a data center.

Storage Cost

Note that the more data or larger the amount of storage, the higher the transaction cost in terms of fuel. However, storage in an Ethereum network is not time bound; it's a one-time payment, and data could be there forever. Also, reading data from the network is free. In later chapters, you will learn how reading and writing to the network work.

The cost of each instruction in a smart contract will limit the amount of storage it uses. Ethereum allows for a theoretically infinite storage space, yet you have to provide gas for every read/write operation carefully. Learning how to build a smart contract in Solidity is easy, but knowing which architecture to adopt and programming using best practices will really help you to create contracts in the most efficient way so you can make the entire ecosystem profitable.

The Entire Ethereum Ecosystem

Now that you know about the blockchain, I'll cover the basics of Ethereum and how its internal mechanisms work. However, few questions still remain unanswered. We all know that storing a huge amount of data on a public Ethereum blockchain would be quite expensive.

So, where should you store your data?

The data stored in smart contracts is safe and easy to access, yet the cost and the structure of the store make it relevant mostly for metadata-related uses because saving real data would be too expensive.

In addition, how do Ethereum nodes participate with each other on a peer-to-peer basis for reaching consensus?

Ethereum has its own messaging protocol called Whisper.

Figure 2-3 is an architecture diagram representing the entire Ethereum ecosystem on a network. The EVM is mostly for running the smart contracts and also for getting a consensus between all participants. Let's find out more about these solutions.

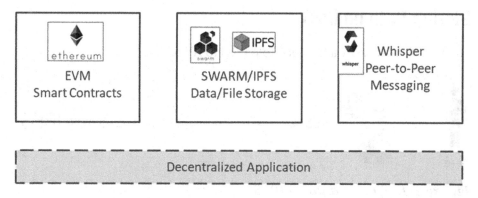

Figure 2-3. *Ethereum ecosystem*

Interplanetary File System

Ethereum is too heavy as well as expensive to store large blobs like images, video, and so on. Hence, some external storage is necessary to store bigger objects. This is where the Interplanetary File System (IPFS) comes into the picture. The Ethereum Dapp can hold a small amount of data, whereas for saving anything more or bigger such as images, word, PDF files, and so on, we can rely on IPFS.

IPFS is a protocol and network designed to create a peer-to-peer method of storing and sharing data. It was initially designed by Juan Benet and is now an open source project developed with help from the community.

If you have heard of the BitTorrent protocol, then IPFS will not be new to you. BitTorrent enables the fast download of large files using minimum Internet bandwidth.

Unlike other download methods, BitTorrent maximizes transfer speed by gathering pieces of the file you want and downloading these pieces simultaneously from people who already have them. IPFS does not entirely follow the BitTorrent protocol but rather takes several good ideas from many other protocols such as Git, SFS, Bitcoin, and the Web, and gathers them all into one package. IPFS connects all computing devices with the same system of files. In some ways, IPFS is similar to the Web.

Storing Data on IPFS

Figure 2-4 shows how a file gets uploaded to IPFS.

Figure 2-4. *Storing data on IPFS*

1. Alice wants to upload a PDF, Word, or image file to IPFS.

2. She puts this PDF, Word, or image file in her working directory.

3. She informs IPFS to add this file, which generates a hash of the file. Note an IPFS hash always starts with "Qm...."

4. Her file is available on the IPFS network.

Note the same is applicable to a file or even to a simple string or integer or Boolean information. For every data piece, what IPFS returns is a hash value.

Sharing Data on IPFS

Now in Figure 2-5 let's see how the same file that is stored on IPFS can be shared with others.

Figure 2-5. *Sharing data on IPFS*

Now if Alice wants to share the file with Bob, what she will do?

1. Alice provides the hash of the file to Bob.

2. Bob uses the hash and calls IPFS for the file.

3. The file is now downloaded at Bob's end.

The issue here is that anyone who can get access to the hash will also be able to get access to the file.

Sharing Data on IPFS by Asymmetric Cryptography

In Figure 2-6, additional security has been introduced via cryptology to encrypt the file so that only authorized people can read it.

Figure 2-6. *Storing data on IPFS*

Alice wants to upload a PDF file to IPFS but wants to restrict the access only to Bob.

1. She puts his PDF file in his working directory and encrypts it with Bob's public key.

2. IPFS generates a hash of the encrypted file, and the encrypted file is available on the IPFS network.

47

3. Bob can retrieve the file by using the hash sent by Alice.

4. Bob decrypts the file using his private key of the public key that was used to encrypt the file.

5. A malicious party cannot decrypt the file because they lack Bob's private key.

IPFS and Ethereum, Brothers in Arms

IPFS is considered the most promising solution for saving data for decentralized applications (see Figure 2-7). Without IPFS, the blockchain would be reduced to any other regular storing mechanism with many limitations.

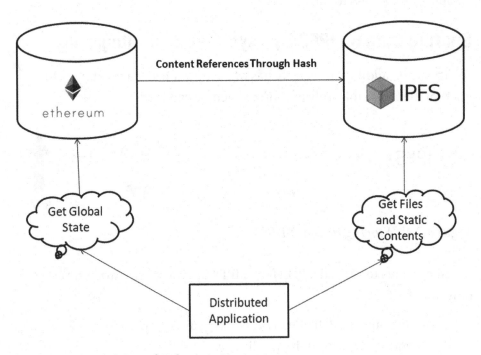

Figure 2-7. *IPFS and Ethereum*

Basically, you store any file in IPFS, and then you store the IPFS hash in the Ethereum contract. Any user with an IPFS node will be able to access the file using that hash.

You can store data, images, the front end, and whatever you want.

IPFS is a protocol that can be used independently and not necessarily in a blockchain. However, in real life, IPFS and the blockchain are a perfect match! With the support of IPFS, data can remain immutable and permanent, and just like any other content databases, you can link the address of the file stored to the Ethereum blockchain. With IPFS, the Ethereum user has to focus only on the contract without having to put the data on the chain itself.

The web site Etherfaces.com is a Dapp built on Ethereum and IPFS.

Swarm

Like IPFS, Swarm is a peer-to-peer data-sharing network. Swarm is completely decentralized service of the Ethereum Web3 stack. Swarm consists of many nodes, and until a single node hosts a piece of data, data sharing goes on. Hence, there is no need for a centralized server.

IPFS vs. Swarm

Both IPFS and Swarm provide an open source solution for efficient decentralized storage for Ethereum DAPPS. Here are a few differences:

- IPFS already serves as a working solution for real-world businesses and has been in production for some time. It is also popular and supported by an enthusiastic user base. Swarm has just recently launched the first stage of a developer testnet.

- You can find many materials related to IPFS videos, documentation, papers, and so on, on the Internet to help you during development. That's not the case for Swarm.

- IPFS scales quite reasonably. Swarm is just starting to be tested on a larger scale.

So, we will continue our development on IPFS; you can watch Swarm as it matures and has related documentations and libraries ready to be used in production.

Whisper

In a decentralized application, where there are participants who are consistently trying to reach a consensus, one-to-one communication between them is vital. That's why Whisper plays a crucial role in the Ethereum ecosystem. Whisper is the "decentralized chat" mechanism on the Ethereum platform that works on a peer-to-peer protocol. In other words, no server is involved in the entire process. So, how does it work? Let's find out.

In the Whisper protocol, as shown in Figure 2-8, every message is routed across the network after encrypting using asymmetric cryptography; in other words, the message is encrypted using the public key of the receiver and is hence safely broadcast over the public network. From node to node, a message keeps moving until it reaches its final destination. Only the owner of the private key that matches with the public key that encrypted the message can decrypt and read it. One more interesting factor is the message sender is not traceable in the Whisper protocol.

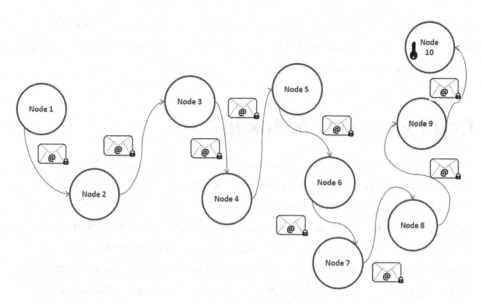

Figure 2-8. *How message transfer works in Whisper*

Whisper is part of the larger Ethereum ecosystem that has nothing to do with the blockchain. Its sole purpose is peer-to-peer message communication. Whisper enables users to share small text information (not files or bigger data) across the same Ethereum network that they use for transactions. Whisper is kind of a distributed hash table where data can be saved in a key-value pair. Here the data to be communicated is the value, and the key refers to the identity of the receiver peer for which the message is sent.

But wait, what is the biggest risk while architecting such a messaging network? Can't someone spam the entire network by sending millions of messages in one go? What mechanism does Whisper use to counter such a possible DDOS attack? Well, it uses a proof-of-work algorithm; messages would be received and further transmitted only if it exceeds a minimum threshold of proof of work and otherwise not. All nodes perform this proof of work on the message to keep the entire network up and running and also spam-free. Though this messaging system is neither super-fast nor in real time, it is completely secure and efficiently broadcasts messages to peers.

Cryptocurrency or Token?

If you want to run a Dapp on a public Ethereum EVM, then you need real ether. Unfortunately, many people think of this part of the business much later when they are done with their coding and about to deploy the smart contract on the main Internet, which would need real currency. It's wise to know the entire ecosystem and plan for it even before you start building out your architecture. You should know how much a transaction will cost you and how much ether you will need to procure from the market for this.

Ether

The cryptocurrency associated with Ethereum is ether. However, rather than just being used as a cryptocurrency, it can be used as a mode of transfer of money against transactions.

Wei

One ether can be divided into many denominations. The smallest denomination (aka base unit) of ether is the wei. Figure 2-9 lists the named denominations and their value in wei.

Unit	Wei Value	Wei
wei	1 wei	1
Kwei (babbage)	1e3 wei	1,000
Mwei (lovelace)	1e6 wei	1,000,000
Gwei (shannon)	1e9 wei	1,000,000,000
microether (szabo)	1e12 wei	1,000,000,000,000
milliether (finney)	1e15 wei	1,000,000,000,000,000
ether	1e18 wei	1,000,000,000,000,000,000

Figure 2-9. *Subunits of ether*

You can find the online conversion rates at `https://etherconverter.online/`.

How to Get Ether

To obtain Ether, you need to do one of the following:

- Be a miner for Ethereum.

- Exchange your Bitcoins for buying ethers or simply by paying your regular fiat currency. Many cryptocurrency exchanges can help.

- Use the user-friendly Mist Ethereum GUI Wallet that as of Beta 6 introduced the ability to purchase ether using the `http://shapeshift.io/` API.

There is a list of cryptocurrency exchanges across the world at `https://www.buybitcoinworldwide.com/cryptocurrency/exchanges/`.

Plan this out early in your project as you will need real ethers to test your Dapp in user acceptance testing and in production when deployed on a public server.

Private Ethereum Blockchains

You now know about ether, gas costs, and mining; yet these are of little significance in the case of a private Ethereum blockchain.

Ethereum can be deployed in public or private blockchain mode. The Ethereum main network is obviously a public blockchain. However, you can spin up your own Ethereum blockchain by creating your own Genesis file and setting up a unique network ID to create a private Ethereum blockchain. Also, you might have to set up strict firewall rules across commonly used RPC ports.

Nowadays, more and more Ethereum projects are deployed on a private blockchain framework where the transaction validator or the miner is the transaction initiator itself and there is no need to procure Ethers to fuel the network. In Chapter 4, I will discuss how to deploy a private Ethereum blockchain and get your business going.

CHAPTER 3

Basic Solidity Programming

As mentioned in Chapter 2, Solidity is the most widely used language for writing smart contracts with Ethereum. Basic Solidity programming is quite easy to learn. It's similar to JavaScript and yet has some features of object-oriented languages such as Java and C++. Hence, some programming experience is desirable before jumping to development in Solidity, although it's not mandatory.

Prerequisites

For learning Solidity programming, you do not need to install any special software on your machine. You just need the following:

- Chrome browser

- High-speed Internet

Remix Browser

The best IDE for learning Solidity is Remix (see Figure 3-1). It is an online browser-based IDE available at http://remix.ethereum.org that comes with a source editor and a file manager as well as with compiling, deploying, and debugging options. While developing, you have to make sure you are connected to the Internet.

© Debajani Mohanty 2018
D. Mohanty, *Ethereum for Architects and Developers*,
https://doi.org/10.1007/978-1-4842-4075-5_3

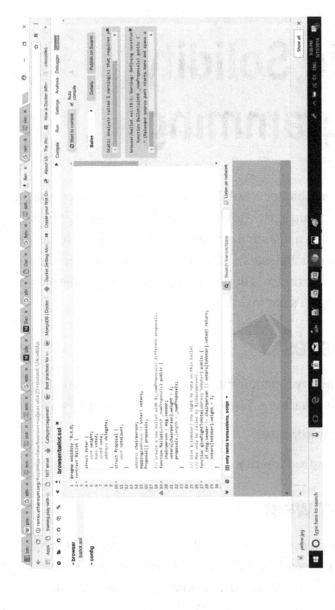

Figure 3-1. Remix online browser

This IDE comes with a default contract named `ballet.sol`, which I will discuss later in the chapter in detail. For the time being, you can click this file on the left side of the screen if it's not open already and then expand it to browse through it. You can also click the + link on the menu to create a new contract. When you write your contract, you can either compile your contract manually by clicking the "Start to compile" button on right side of the Compile tab or click the "Auto compile" check box to get it done on the fly.

If something goes wrong in the code, you will see a red box with an X next to the line in the source (see Figure 3-2).

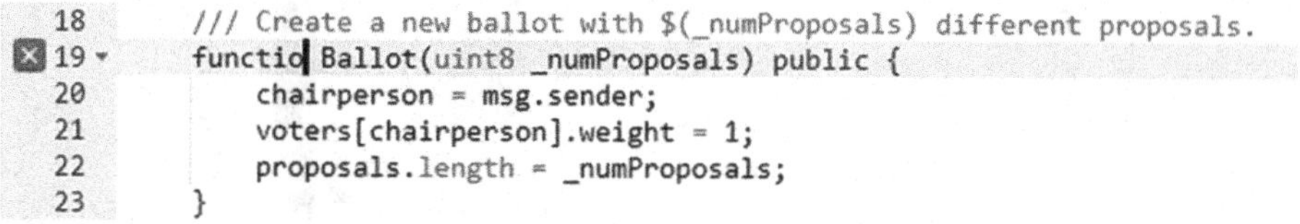

```
18        /// Create a new ballot with $(_numProposals) different proposals.
19 ▾      function Ballot(uint8 _numProposals) public {
20            chairperson = msg.sender;
21            voters[chairperson].weight = 1;
22            proposals.length = _numProposals;
23        }
```

Figure 3-2. *Compilation error in Remix*

Sometimes you can also see many yellow warnings, but they will not stop you from executing the code (see Figure 3-3).

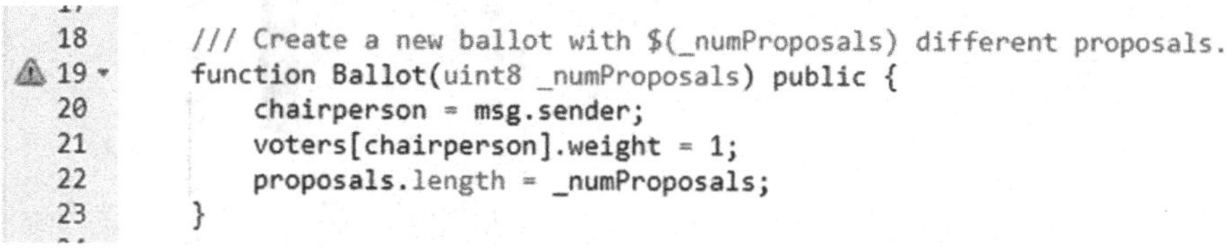

```
18        /// Create a new ballot with $(_numProposals) different proposals.
19 ▾      function Ballot(uint8 _numProposals) public {
20            chairperson = msg.sender;
21            voters[chairperson].weight = 1;
22            proposals.length = _numProposals;
23        }
```

Figure 3-3. *Warnings in Remix*

Deploying Contracts in Remix

Once your contract is compiled successfully, you can click the Run tab on the right side and choose an option from the drop-down. Choose JavaScript VM, which is the default mode when you don't use Remix with Mist or MetaMask (covered later), as shown in Figure 3-4. It comes with five accounts, each with gas limit of 3,000,000.

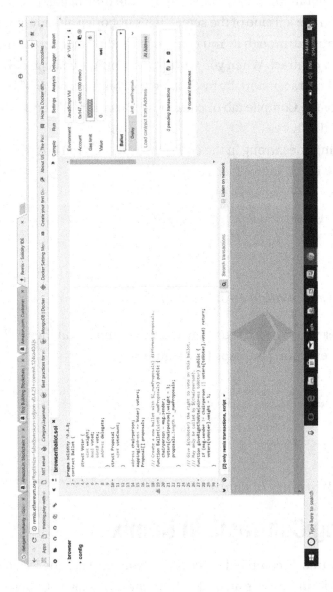

Figure 3-4. Deploying a smart contract in Remix using the JavaScript VM

Solidity File Details

Let's find out more about some Solidity features before starting programming.

Extension

A Solidity file is always saved with an .sol extension.

File Storage

The file will be available on your Chrome browser unless you either delete it or clear the cache. To avoid accidental deletion of the file from browser storage, you can use Remixd, which enables you to store and sync files in the browser with your local computer. For further details, refer to http:// remix.readthedocs.io/en/latest/tutorial_remixd_filesystem.html.

Application Binary Interface

Every contract has an application binary interface (ABI), which is pretty much like an API that works as an interface between the high-level language and the lower-level binary code that gets processed by dumb computers. The ABI consists of the following:

- All function names

- Input and output types of functions

- All event names and their parameters

If you open the Remix browser at http://remix.ethereum.org, open the default ballot.sol, click its Compile tab, and then click the Details button, a pop-up appears. You can find the ABI section under it, as shown in Figure 3-5. Click the rectangular area to copy the ABI, as shown in Listing 3-1.

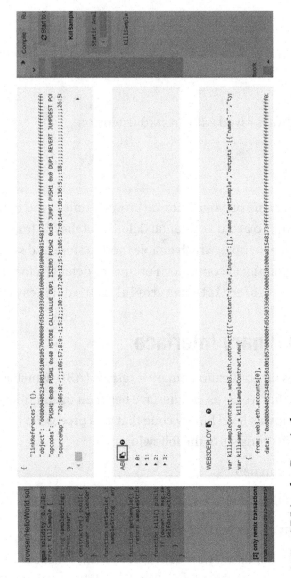

Figure 3-5. ABI in the Remix browser

Listing 3-1. The ABI File

```
[
    {
        "constant": false,
        "inputs": [],
        "name": "kill",
        "outputs": [],
        "payable": false,
        "stateMutability": "nonpayable",
        "type": "function"
    },
    {
        "constant": false,
        "inputs": [
            {
                "name": "anyString",
                "type": "string"
            }
        ],
        "name": "setSample",
        "outputs": [],
        "payable": false,
        "stateMutability": "nonpayable",
        "type": "function"
    },
    {
        "inputs": [],
        "payable": false,
        "stateMutability": "nonpayable",
        "type": "constructor"
    },
```

```
{
    "constant": true,
    "inputs": [],
    "name": "getSample",
    "outputs": [
        {
            "name": "",
            "type": "string"
        }
    ],
    "payable": false,
    "stateMutability": "view",
    "type": "function"
}
]
```

Import Statement

Just like with Java and JavaScript, you can import other files within a Solidity file and use a symbol for that file. You also have to specify the path of the file properly, as shown in Listing 3-2.

Listing 3-2. Importing Part of a Solidity File

```
import "filename" as symbolName;
```

Version

The first line of code in a Solidity file always starts with a pragma annotation where you fix the compiler to a particular version so that if the version of Solidity gets updated, it will not affect compilation leading to incompatibility issues (see Listing 3-3).

Listing 3-3. Pragma Annotation

```
pragma solidity ^0.4.0;
contract MyContract{
}
```

Variables

In Solidity, variables are either at the state level and at the local level. The state-level variables are global to the Solidity file, whereas local ones are valid only for the function within which it's declared.

The default location for storing function input and output parameters is memory; the default for local variables is storage in the EVM. However, you can always override this part.

Just like Java, Solidity too is a statically typed language, where the data type of variables have to be declared at compilation time. The variables can be broadly divided into two types, by value and by reference.

By Value

By value variables are the simple data types where variables are copied with their values. Here are few types explained.

Integers

Integers in Solidity can be either signed (i.e., int) or unsigned (i.e., uint) type. By default the size is 256 bits; in other words, by default an int is int256, and uint is uint256 bits. You can have other sizes such as int8/uint8, int16/uint16, int32/uint32, and son on, up to int256/uint256.

Fixed Numbers

A number can be of a fixed value by using the fixed keyword.

Boolean

In Solidity, *bool* stands for a Boolean value that is either true or false. You can do logical operations like "or," "and," "equal to," "not equal to," and so on, to get a Boolean value.

Byte

In Solidity, a byte is a fixed-size byte array.

Enum

An enum represents a fixed number of predefined constant values and must have at least one. They are greatly helpful when you have unmodified related data, such as days of a week or holidays in a year. Listing 3-4 shows an example.

Listing 3-4. SimpleEnum.sol

```
pragma solidity ^0.4.4;

contract SimpleEnum {
enumSomeData {DEFAULT,ONE,TWO}
SomeDatasomeData;

constructor () internal  {
     someData = SomeData.DEFAULT;
  }

function  setValues(uint _value) public payable{
     require(uint(SomeData.TWO) >= _value);
     someData = SomeData(_value);
  }
```

```
functiongetValue() public constant returns (uint){
        returnuint(someData);
  }

}
```

Address

An address is a type that saves an account address on an Ethereum node. Addresses can be useful, as you will learn in case studies and examples. Using an address's balance and transfer functions, you can transfer an amount from one to another address on Ethereum nodes.

By Reference

Passing by reference means while copying one variable to another, the actual pointer to the memory location of the first variable is passed to the other. Now both the original variable and the new variable point to the same memory location, which means if one's value changes, then the other will be affected. But why? Well, sometimes you have complex data more than 256 bits in size, which would be too expensive to store in a traditional manner. You can create a complex type and store it in memory or storage as per your needs. Arrays and structs are two complex data types passed by reference.

Array

An array can be created with a fixed length that you assign at the time of declaration, or it can have a variable-length type. Also, an array can be of several data types such as byte, string, int, uint, and so on.

Struct

A struct is the most interesting complex data type because it can further be comprised of many other simple data types, arrays, and mappings.

String

In Solidity, a string is a type passed by reference. Strange, isn't it?

The string data type is used for arbitrary-length UTF-8 and also costs more gas when compared to the fixed-size types of bytes1 to bytes32.

Mappings

Mappings are always state variables and similar to hash tables in Java where key-value pair data is stored (see Listing 3-5).

Where does this data get stored?

- By default state variables are always stored in a storage data location.

- Mappings are stored in a storage data location; this can't be overridden.

- By default local variables of value types within a function are stored in a memory data location.

Listing 3-5. MyContract.sol

```
pragma solidity ^0.4.0;
contract MyContract {

function myFunction(uint i) public {
..
}

}
```

But that can be overridden to be saved to storage instead, as shown here:

```
pragma solidity ^0.4.0;
contract MyContract {
```

```
function myFunction(uint storage i) public {
..
}

}
```

- By default reference type variables are stored in a storage data location.

- The reference type variables can override the default setting to be stored in a memory data location instead.

I will discuss different data storage locations in more detail later in the book.

Solidity Comments

Like Java, Solidity has two ways to add comments, as one-liners or as multiliners (see Listing 3-6).

Listing 3-6. Comments

```
//This is an one-line comment
/*
This is a
Multiline comment
*/
```

Function

Functions are the locations where you can have the business logic and also can save and retrieve data (see Listing 3-7).

Listing 3-7. A Function

```solidity
pragma solidity ^0.4.0;
contract MyContract{
    function myFunction() public {
}
}
```

A function can have different visibilities that will be discussed later. Also, a function can optionally return one or more values.

```solidity
contract MultiReturner {
    function getData() constant returns (bytes32, bytes32) {
        bytes32 a = "abcd";
        bytes32 b = "wxyz";
        return (a, b);
    }

    function getDynamicData()returns (bytes, bytes) {
        bytes a;
        a.push('a');
        a.push('b');
        a.push('c');
        bytes b;
        b.push('x');
        b.push('y');
        b.push('z');
        return (a, b);
    }
}
```

How can you retrieve this data? Well, you can call the previous contract from another contract, as shown in Listing 3-8.

Listing 3-8. UsesMultiReturner.sol

```
contract UsesMultiReturner {
    function doIt() {
        mr = MultiReturner(0x1234);

        // this will work
        var (a, b) = mr.getData();

        // this won't work
        var (a, b) = mr.getDynamicData();
    }
}
```

Fallback Function

A Solidity file can have exactly one unnamed function with the keyword payable, which is known as a *fallback function* (see Listing 3-9).

Listing 3-9. Fallback Function

```
pragma solidity ^0.4.0;

contract Fallback {

    function () payable {

    }

}
```

This signifies that anyone on an Ethereum blockchain can interact with this contract address without specifying the function name or input arguments.

Function Modifiers

Just like annotations in Java, function modifiers are used to induce business logic declaratively (see Listing 3-10).

Listing 3-10. Function Modifiers

```
pragma solidity ^0.4.11;

contract Purchase {
    address public seller;

    modifier onlySeller() { // Modifier
        require(msg.sender == seller);
        _;
    }

    function abort() public onlySeller { // Modifier usage
        // ...
    }
}
```

The _; in onlySeller() signifies that the function that uses onlySeller(), which is the abort() function here, will be executed after the onlySeller() function is executed.

Constructor

A constructor is a function with the same name as a contract. Every contract can optionally have one constructor in it. However, unlike Java, the constructor can't be overloaded. The constructor is invoked only once when the contract is created. Hence, you can keep any kind of initialization code within it (see Listing 3-11).

Listing 3-11. A Constructor

```
pragma solidity ^0.4.0;
contract MyContract{
    function MyContract() {
}
}
```

However, this pattern is deprecated, and though you can still write this way, the compiler will throw the warning shown in Figure 3-6 for the pattern as well as the visibility.

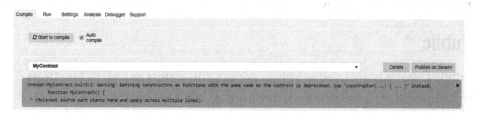

Figure 3-6. *Warning in Remix for constructor*

So, it's better write the pattern shown in Listing 3-12.

Listing 3-12. MyContract.sol

```
pragma solidity ^0.4.0;

contract MyContract{

    constructor() public {

    }
}
```

Visibility

For functions, there are four visibility types: external, public, internal, and private. The default is public.

For state variables, there are only two visibility types: public and internal. The default is internal.

External

A contract can be called from another contract provided the external contract already knows the calling contract by using the external keyword part of the contract name.

Public

Public keywords are used mostly in getters and setters as well as functions that you want to invoke on the contract directly. They can also be used against state variables.

Internal

The visibility is only from within the current contract or contracts deriving from it.

Private

The visibility is only for the contract they are defined in and not in derived contracts.

Getter and Setter

Listing 3-13 creates a constructor that sets an unsigned integer as well as a setter and getter.

Listing 3-13. Getter and Setter

```solidity
pragma solidity ^0.4.0;

contract MyFirstContract {
    string private name;
    uint private age;

    function setName(string newName) public {
        name = newName;
    }

    function getName() public view returns (string) {
        return name;
    }

    function setAge(uint newAge) public {
        age = newAge;
    }

    function getAge() public view returns (uint) {
        return age;
    }
}
```

Now compile and deploy the contract. Set the name and age, as shown in Figure 3-7; note that for string you must use apostrophes.

Figure 3-7. *Testing the setter function in the Remix browser*

Keep an eye on the web console just below the source editor (see Figure 3-8).

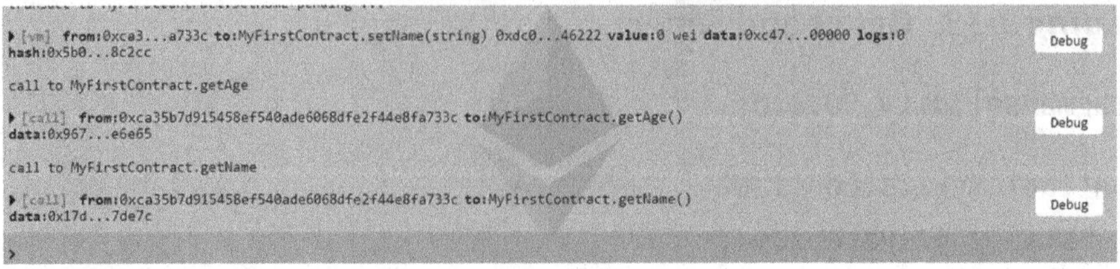

Figure 3-8. *Remix console*

Expand each section to check whether there is any issue and also different properties such as status, gas cost, and so on. It also gives you the facility to debug, which I will discuss later in the book (see Figure 3-9).

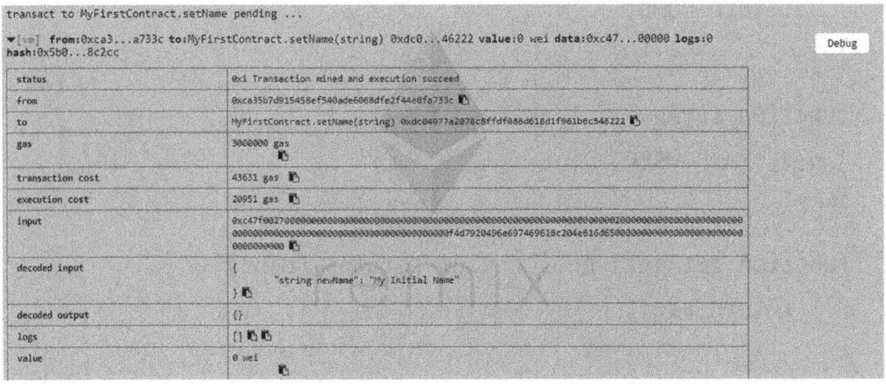

Figure 3-9. *Remix console showing different properties*

Error Handling: throw, revert(), assert(), require()

In an earlier version of Solidity, throw was used for handling error conditions (see Listing 3-14).

Listing 3-14. throw Operation

```
contract MyContract {
    address owner;
    function checkUser(){
```

```
    if (msg.sender != owner) { throw; }
    // do something only the owner should be allowed to do
  }
}
```

throw is more of an operation than a function. If the checkUser()
function is called by anyone other than owner, the function will throw an
error, returning an invalid opcode error, undoing all the state changes, and
using up all the remaining gas.

However, in a recent version of Solidity, throw is deprecated, and
soon it might be eliminated for use, mostly because it's expensive. The
new functions assert(), require(), and revert() provide the same
functionality, with a much finer as well as cleaner syntax.

The same error condition now can be handled by using a call to
revert()(see Listing 3-15).

Listing 3-15. revert()

```
if(msg.sender != owner) { revert(); }
```

Or it can be handled by using an assert() check, as shown in
Listing 3-16.

Listing 3-16. assert()

```
assert(msg.sender == owner);
```

Or it can be handled by using a require() statement, which you
already saw before, as shown in Listing 3-17.

Listing 3-17. require()

```
require(msg.sender == owner);
```

Again, note that when your contract throws an error, it uses up any remaining gas; however, revert() and require() would return the gas value, which is beneficial for you. Unlike these two, assert(), however, consumes the gas. Then why would you use assert()? There are some fundamental differences between the three.

- The require() function is used to validate a particular piece of business logic. The same is true for the revert() function.

- The assert() function has more to do with the runtime value of a parameter. It's used to validate the state after some change, and it's used toward the end of the function. You have to use it wisely.

Function with No Gas Cost

The constant keyword in the getter function denotes that there is no transaction associated with this function, and hence no gas will be consumed. In fact, a constant state variable is evaluated every time it is called. However, in the latest version, it's deprecated, and instead you can use pure or view. These keywords denote that there is no transactional activity in that function.

In earlier versions, you would apply the constant modifier to indicate that a function doesn't change the storage state in any way. Listing 3-18 shows an example.

Listing 3-18. UseConstant.sol

```
pragma solidity ^0.4.16;

contract UseConstant {

    string greeting;
```

```
function UseConstant() public {
    greeting = "Hello";
}

function SayHello() public constant returns(string says) {
    return greeting;
}
}
```

Constant

The constant keyword indicates that network verification won't be necessary. Callers receive return values (quickly, from local storage and processing) instead of transaction hashes.

Starting with solc 0.4.17, constant is deprecated in favor of two new and more specific modifiers.

View

This is generally the replacement for constant. It indicates that the function will not alter the storage state in any way.

Pure

This is even more restrictive, indicating that it won't even read the storage state.

A pure function might look something like the contrived example in Listing 3-19.

Listing 3-19. A pure function

```
function returnTrue() public pure returns(bool) {
    return true;
}
```

Data Storage

We all know that Solidity compiles to smart contracts that run on the Ethereum Virtual Machine. Internally the EVM uses three different types of memory location for saving smart contracts and related data: storage, memory, and stack.

Storage

Storage is the permanent memory of every account where all the contract state variables reside. Data is stored in a key-value pair that maps 256-bit words to 256-bit words. Any contract can read and update data only from its own storage but not from others. It's expensive to use.

Memory

Memory is limited to reads at the 256-bit width, while writing can be either 8 or 256 bits wide. It is used to hold temporary values. Memory cannot be used at the contract level. It is erased between (external) function calls and is cheaper to use.

Calldata

Almost like memory, this is a nonmodifiable, nonpersistent data location where function arguments are stored.

Stack

If you want to store a small amount of information at a low gas cost, then use a stack. In addition to arrays and structs, all other local variables of most value types are stored in stack (see Listing 3-20).

Listing 3-20. Storage.sol

```solidity
pragma solidity ^0.4.0;

contract Storage {

    uint[] private vars;

    function saveToStack() {
        uint myVal1 = 1;
        uint myVal2 = 2;
    }

    function saveToMemory() {
        string memory myString = "test";
    }

    function saveToStorage() {
        vars.push(2);
        vars.push(3);
    }

}
```

Events

Events are useful for logging activities. An emit keyword is used to call events explicitly (see Listing 3-21).

Listing 3-21. MyEvent.sol

```solidity
pragma solidity ^0.4.0;

contract MyEvent {
    event HighestBidIncreased(address bidder, uint amount);
    // Event
```

```
function MyEvent() {
}

function bid() public payable {
    // ...
    emit HighestBidIncreased(msg.sender, msg.value);
    // Triggering event
}
}
```

Object-Oriented Approach

In Solidity a contract is equivalent to a class in Java. Also, just like Java and C++, Solidity comes with many object-oriented features. Some of its features are inheritance, polymorphism, abstraction, encapsulation, method overloading, and so on.

Encapsulation

State variables are internal or private, and functions are public by default. This you already observed in the "Visibility" section. Figure 3-10 shows some sample code.

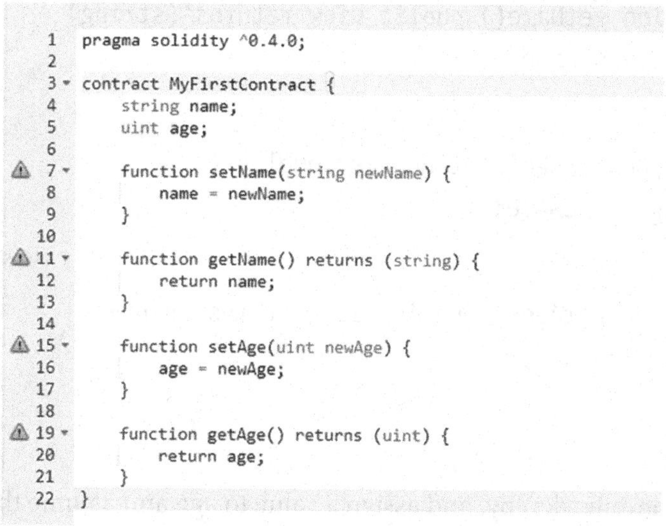

```
 1   pragma solidity ^0.4.0;
 2
 3 ▾ contract MyFirstContract {
 4       string name;
 5       uint age;
 6
⚠ 7 ▾     function setName(string newName) {
 8           name = newName;
 9       }
10
⚠11 ▾     function getName() returns (string) {
12           return name;
13       }
14
⚠15 ▾     function setAge(uint newAge) {
16           age = newAge;
17       }
18
⚠19 ▾     function getAge() returns (uint) {
20           return age;
21       }
22 }
```

Figure 3-10. A simple contract in Remix

Here the compiler throws warnings because I have not mentioned visibility against the setter functions and also marked the getters as view, which are best practices. Update this example to the code shown in Listing 3-22 and the warnings will go away.

Listing 3-22. MyFirstContract.sol

```
pragma solidity ^0.4.0;

contract MyFirstContract {
    string private name;
    uint private age;

    function setName(string newName) public {
        name = newName;
    }
```

```
function getName() public view returns (string) {
    return name;
}

function setAge(uint newAge) public {
    age = newAge;
}

function getAge() public view returns (uint) {
    return age;
}
}
```

Now compile, deploy, and assign a value to age and a name through the setName() and setAge() buttons (see Figure 3-11). Then click the get buttons to check whether they are properly assigned. Do not forget to use double quotes for assigning string values.

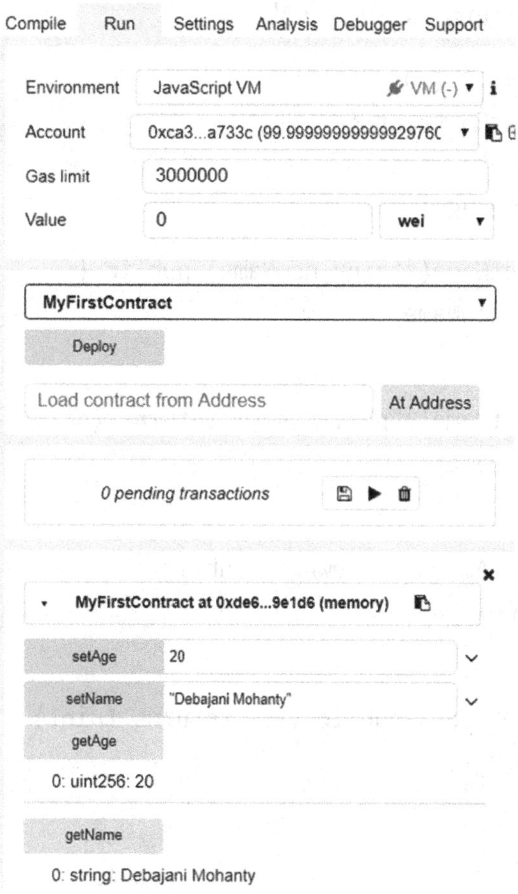

Compile   Run   Settings   Analysis   Debugger   Support

Environment   JavaScript VM   ⚡ VM (-) ▼ ⓘ

Account   0xca3...a733c (99.99999999999992976C ▼ 🗐 ⓔ

Gas limit   3000000

Value   0   wei   ▼

MyFirstContract   ▼

Deploy

Load contract from Address   At Address

0 pending transactions   🖫 ▶ 🗑

                                                          ✖

▾   MyFirstContract at 0xde6...9e1d6 (memory)   🗐

setAge   20   ⌄

setName   "Debajani Mohanty"   ⌄

getAge

0: uint256: 20

getName

0: string: Debajani Mohanty

Figure 3-11. *Deploying and testing in Remix*

Inheritance

Inheritance is not a new concept for Java or C++ programmers. It gives
you the ability to inherit or acquire the properties and functions of other
classes so that you do not have to write the same piece of functionality in
many different places (see Listing 3-23).

Listing 3-23. MyFirstContract.sol

```solidity
pragma solidity ^0.4.0;
contract MyFirstContract {
    string private name;
    uint private age;

    function setName(string newName) public {
        name = newName;
    }

    function getName() public view returns (string) {
        return name;
    }

    function setAge(uint newAge) public {
        age = newAge;
    }

    function getAge() public view returns (uint) {
        return age;
    }
}

contract MysecondContract is MyFirstContract{

    string private name;

    function setName(string newName) public {
        name = "Test";
    }

    function getName() public view returns (string) {
        return name;
    }

}
```

Now compile and deploy the second contract named MysecondContract and set any value through the setName() function. getName() will always give you the value you have assigned to name through the MySecondContract contract. Here, setAge() and getAge() are inherited from the parent class and will work as before.

Polymorphism

Just like C++, Solidity supports polymorphism through multiple inheritance.

Abstraction

Abstraction is the process used to hide certain details and show only the essential features of the object. In other words, it deals with the outside view of an object. Abstraction is implemented in Solidity through abstract contracts as well as interfaces.

Abstract Contract

Unlike Java, Solidity contracts do not need an abstract keyword to be marked abstract. Rather, any contract that has at least one unimplemented function is treated as abstract in Solidity. An abstract contract can be neither compiled nor deployed unless it has an implementing contract (see Listing 3-24).

Listing 3-24. MyAbstract.sol

```
pragma solidity ^0.4.0;

contract MyAbstract {
    function myAbstractFunction() public pure returns (string);
}
```

```
contract MyImplementation is MyAbstract {
    function myAbstractFunction() public pure returns (string)
{ return "Test"; }
}
```

Just like Java, if a contract inherits an abstract contract and does not implement all the unimplemented functions, then that contract will be considered abstract as well (see Figure 3-12). An abstract contract can have both implemented and unimplemented functions.

***Figure 3-12.** Remix showing error for unimplemented functions*

Please note while deploying, you should choose the implementer contract because the abstract contract cannot be deployed (see Figure 3-13).

Figure 3-13. *In Remix, choose the implementer contract.*

Interface

Similar to Java, interfaces can have only unimplemented functions. Also, they are neither compiled nor deployed unless there is a implanting contract (see Listing 3-25).

Listing 3-25. Interface in Solidity

```
pragma solidity ^0.4.0;

interface MyInterface {
    function myFunction(string) returns (string);
}

contract MyImplementation is MyInterface {
    function myFunction(string str) returns (string) { return
str; }
}
```

In Solidity, inheritance and interfaces are realized in the same way in the implementing contract.

Function Overloading

Like Java, multiple functions can have the same name with different argument types (see Listing 3-26).

Listing 3-26. Multiple Functions with same name

```
pragma solidity ^0.4.16;

contract A {
    function f(uint _in) public pure returns (uint) {
        out = 1;
    }

    function f(uint _in, bytes32 _key) public pure returns
(uint) {
        out = 2;
    }
}
```

Libraries

A library is synonymous to a contract with a few variations. A library doesn't have any storage and cannot hold ether. Sometimes it is helpful to think of a library as a singleton in the EVM, a piece of code that can be called from any contract without the need to deploy it again. It is mostly utilized as a common utility file that contracts can import and use (see Listing 3-27).

Listing 3-27. MyLibrary.sol

```
pragma solidity ^0.4.0;

library MyLibrary {
```

```solidity
function addTen(uint age) public pure returns (uint) {
    return age + 10;
}
}

contract TestLibrary{

    function testIncrementByTen(uint age) public pure returns
(uint) {
        return MyLibrary.addTen(age);
    }
}
```

End a Contract

A contract can be discarded by calling the kill() function that internally calls the selfdestruct(address) function. Providing an address as the parameter to selfdestruct lets you transfer the remaining funds to the contract on the address. You must always think about who the authorized person is that can kill the contract, or it could be accidentally be deleted by anyone (see Listing 3-28).

Listing 3-28. KillSample.sol

```solidity
pragma solidity ^0.4.18;
contract KillSample {

    string sampleString;
    address owner;

    constructor() public {
        owner = msg.sender;
    }
```

```
    function setSample( string anyString) public {
        sampleString = anyString;
    }

    function getSample() public view returns(string){
        return sampleString;
    }
function kill() public {
assert(owner == msg.sender); // We check who is calling
selfdestruct(owner); //Destruct the contract

    }
}
```

Now compile and deploy the contract. Set some value through setSample() and retrieve the same through getSample(). Now click the kill() function and then try to retrieve again through getSample(). It will throw the error shown in Figure 3-14.

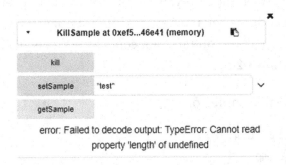

Figure 3-14. *Remix shows an error because the contract has already been destroyed*

After executing the kill() function, it will not be possible to interact with it anymore. If you try to get or set any variable it would throw error.

Solidity, Bytecode, and Opcode

Solidity, like Java or C++, is a high-level language that gets run on the EVM after being translated to bytecode, a low-level language that the EVM understands (see Figure 3-15).

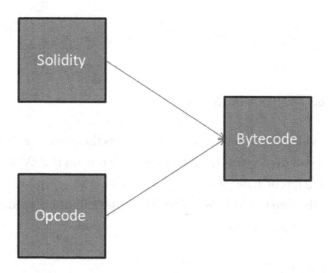

Figure 3-15. *Relationship between Solidity, opcode, and bytecode*

For example, if you open the Remix browser and click the Details button in the default `ballot.sol` file, you will find the bytecode shown in Figure 3-16.

```
WEB3DEPLOY 📋 ❷

var _numProposals = /* var of type uint8 here */ ;
var ballotContract = web3.eth.contract([{"constant":false,"inputs":[{"name":"to","type":"address"}],"name":"delegate"
var ballot = ballotContract.new(
   _numProposals,
   {
     from: web3.eth.accounts[0],
     data: '0x6080604052348015610010057600080fd5b5060405160208061087c833981018060405281019080805190602001909291905050(
     gas: '4700000'
   }, function (e, contract){
   console.log(e, contract);
   if (typeof contract.address !== 'undefined') {
        console.log('Contract mined! address: ' + contract.address + ' transactionHash: ' + contract.transactionHash
   }
})
```

Figure 3-16. *Bytecode in Remix*

Here the value for data that begins with 0x is the bytecode. It also signifies that you deploy this hexadecimal bytecode on the EVM with a recommended gas of 4,700,000.

You can also see the opcode, which is low-level human-readable language, as shown in Figure 3-17.

```
RUNTIME BYTECODE 📋 ❷
{
    "linkReferences": {},
    "object": "6080604052600436106100625760003757c010000000000000000000000000000000000000000000000000000000900463ffff
    "opcodes": "PUSH1 0x80 PUSH1 0x40 MSTORE PUSH1 0x4 CALLDATASIZE LT PUSH2 0x62 JUMPI PUSH1 0x0 CALLDATALOAD PUSH29
    "sourceMap": "24:2138:0:-;;;;;;;;;;;;;;;;;;;;;;;;;;;;;;;;;;;;;;867:577;;8:9:-1;5:2;;;30:1;27;20:12;5:2;867:577:0
}
◄ ▓                                                                                                                  ▶
```

Figure 3-17. *Opcodes in Remix*

Assembly Language

Instead of using Solidity, the whole contract can be written in low-level assembly language using opcode.

Assembly language is far more complex and difficult to write and maintain. Why then use in-line assembly instead of Solidity?

- You get fine-grained control of code.

- The gas cost is phenomenally less than Solidity.

However, in most cases, usage of Assembly language should be avoided as they overlook many security features that have been implemented in Solidity.

Running on Remix

Now let's start learning your first program, ballot.sol, which is available in the Remix browser (Listing 3-29).

- Here declare a struct called Voter that is a complex type consisting of the weight of a vote, a Boolean voted, the address of the voter, and an index called vote.

- You have an address type called chairperson.

- You have a mapping where you map an address with a voter.

- You also create an array of proposals where each proposal is a complex type struct.

In the constructor Ballot, you initialize the chairperson as the message sender with weight 1. You also create a list of proposals. In the giveRightToVote() function, you check whether the message sender is not chairperson and whether voters have not voted yet and then assign voters a weight. Then the delegate() function delegates your vote to the voter $(to) after a couple of validations such as the message sender is not the to address and has not voted (see Listing 3-29).

Listing 3-29. Ballot.sol

```
pragma solidity ^0.4.0;
contract Ballot {

    struct Voter {
        uint weight;
        bool voted;
        uint8 vote;
        address delegate;
    }
    struct Proposal {
        uint voteCount;
    }

    address chairperson;
    mapping(address => Voter) voters;
    Proposal[] proposals;

    /// Create a new ballot with $(_numProposals) different
        proposals.
    function Ballot(uint8 _numProposals) public {
        chairperson = msg.sender;
        voters[chairperson].weight = 1;
        proposals.length = _numProposals;
    }

    /// Give $(toVoter) the right to vote on this ballot.
    /// May only be called by $(chairperson).
    function giveRightToVote(address toVoter) public {
        if (msg.sender != chairperson || voters[toVoter].voted)
        return;
        voters[toVoter].weight = 1;
    }
```

```solidity
/// Delegate your vote to the voter $(to).
function delegate(address to) public {
    Voter storage sender = voters[msg.sender];
    // assigns reference
    if (sender.voted) return;
    while (voters[to].delegate != address(0) && voters[to].
    delegate != msg.sender)
        to = voters[to].delegate;
    if (to == msg.sender) return;
    sender.voted = true;
    sender.delegate = to;
    Voter storage delegateTo = voters[to];
    if (delegateTo.voted)
        proposals[delegateTo.vote].voteCount += sender.
        weight;
    else
        delegateTo.weight += sender.weight;
}

/// Give a single vote to proposal $(toProposal).
function vote(uint8 toProposal) public {
    Voter storage sender = voters[msg.sender];
    if (sender.voted || toProposal >= proposals.length)
    return;
    sender.voted = true;
    sender.vote = toProposal;
    proposals[toProposal].voteCount += sender.weight;
}

function winningProposal() public constant returns (uint8
_winningProposal) {
    uint256 winningVoteCount = 0;
    for (uint8 prop = 0; prop < proposals.length; prop++)
```

```
        if (proposals[prop].voteCount > winningVoteCount) {
            winningVoteCount = proposals[prop].voteCount;
            _winningProposal = prop;
        }
    }
}
```

Here are some of the Solidity features used in this program:

- In the first line, `pragma solidity ^0.4.0;`, you set the version of Solidity.

- You have used different variable types as such as unit, unit8, address, bool, and so on.

- `Voter` is a struct or a composite object that can have many other objects within it.

- The function `delegate` has an address as input that points to a node on the Ethereum network.

- `chairperson` is the address of the owner of the contract that you have associated to `msg.sender` in the constructor `Ballot`.

- `voters` is a mapping of the address to `Voter` structs, so you get a voter by looking up their address in that map. If a voter isn't found, it'll return a `Voter` struct with default empty values.

- `proposals` is an array of the proposals, referenced by an integer index where every `Proposal` is another struct that contains `voteCount`, an unsigned integer.

Here the function `Ballot()` is actually the constructor that has the same name as the contract. Here you do all initialization that is needed.

Debugging on Remix

Now let's debug the same storage Solidity file that we just explored. Now I have added an assert statement at the end of each of these functions (see Listing 3-30).

Listing 3-30. Debugging

```solidity
pragma solidity ^0.4.0;

contract Storage {
    uint[] private vars;

    function saveToStack() {
        uint myVal1 = 1;
        uint myVal2 = 2;
        assert(myVal1 == myVal2);
    }

    function saveToMemory() {
        string memory myString = "test";
        assert(bytes(myString).length == 10);
    }

    function aveToStorage() {
        vars.push(2);
        vars.push(3);
        assert(vars.length == 4);
    }

}
```

Open the Remix browser and compile the file. Now click the Run tab and deploy using the Deploy tab (see Figure 3-18).

Figure 3-18.   Deploying Storage.sol

You can see the names of all the three functions on the right side. Click the first one, saveToStack(), and you will see an exception in the console (see Figure 3-19).

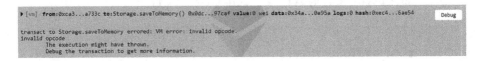

Figure 3-19.   Remix console

Click the Debug button to launch the debugger. Now on the right side, you will see different sections (see Figure 3-20).

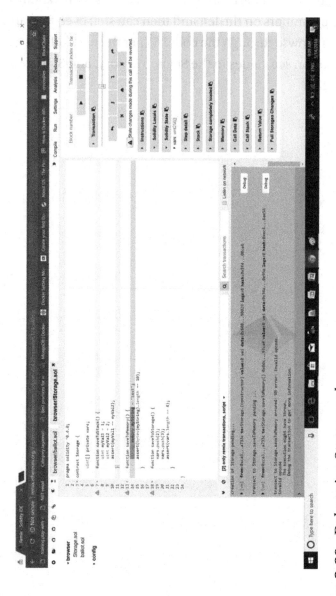

Figure 3-20. Debugging Storage.sol

The Transaction section comes with a glide bar that helps you browse through different parts of the code. You can set breakpoints here by clicking line numbers on the left and then can step over, forward, or backward to browse through the code. As per the method you are debugging, you can see values in the Stack, Memory, and Storage sections (see Figure 3-21).

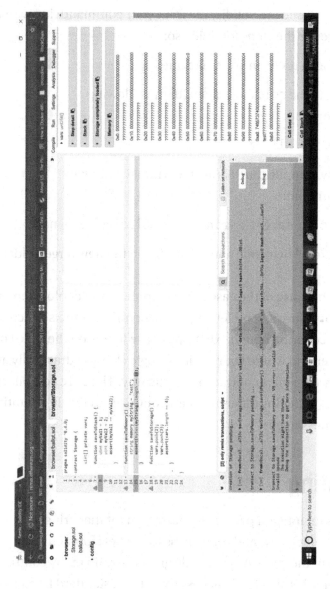

Figure 3-21. Remix showing values in the Stack, Memory, and Storage sections in Storage.sol

Running on the solc Compiler

You can also compile the Solidity file from your command line with a `solc` compiler. Here are the steps for doing so:

1. Install a node on your machine.

2. Install the `solc` compiler with the following command:

   ```
   npm install -g solc
   ```

3. Now compile the Solidity file with the following command:

   ```
   solc -o target --bin --abi<solidity file name>
   ```

This will create bytecode and an ABI file in the new target folder it has created.

However, because of the ease of development and deployment, more and more people are now preferring to use Remix over the `solc` compiler. There is one scenario, though, where you have to rely on the `solc` compiler. Consider a scenario where your business logic changes drastically and you cannot deploy the smart contract in a static way. The `solc` compiler gives you the option to deploy different smart contracts on the fly at runtime as per your business needs.

Unit Testing

Unit testing is an integral part of any development that brings transparency, efficiency, and robustness to the development and maintenance of the code. As your code grows beyond many contracts and many functions, it's absolutely necessary to use a standard framework that comes with superior features such as an automated test suite, timer, report generator, and so on.

There are currently four primary frameworks available that can accelerate your development of Dapps and also facilitate writing unit tests for your contracts. I will cover some in future chapters.

Embark

This is the framework with the widest adoption. This will be covered in Chapter 7.

Web site: `https://embark.readthedocs.io/en/2.6.6/`
Tests: JavaScript via Mocha

Truffle

Truffle is a popular framework; this option seems good for projects because it comes with a built-in feature to test smart contracts. This will be covered in Chapter 7.

Web site: `http://truffleframework.com/docs/getting_started/solidity-tests`
Tests: Mocha

Dapp

Dapp provides command-line functionalities to build, test, deploy, and transact with smart contracts on an Ethereum network.

Web site: `https://dapp.tools/dapp/`
Tests: Solidity

Populus

Populus is another framework to develop smart contracts on the Ethereum blockchain.

Web site: `http://populus.readthedocs.org/en/latest/`
Tests: py.test

CHAPTER 4

Deploying Smart Contracts

Now that you are proficient in smart contract development using Solidity,
let's deploy a contract on an Ethereum network. Deployment can be done
in many ways.

- *Deploy in Remix with the JavaScript VM*: This is
  something you have already done.

- *Ganache*: Formerly known as TestRPC, Ganache is
  a local private setup running on your machine for
  development and unit testing.

- *Ropsten/Kovan/Rinkeby test network and MetaMask*:
  These are Ethereum clients used for functional testing.

- *Truffle Suite*: Truffle Suite is a development and testing
  framework for smart contracts on Ethereum. This will
  be discussed later in the book in detail.

Local Ethereum Testing with Ganache

TestRPC is a Node.js-based Ethereum client for client testing and
development. It offers a private blockchain network that runs only on
your own machine without connecting to any other node in the Ethereum

network; however, it imitates the properties of a test or live Ethereum network. Also, it's a fast, flexible, painless way to emulate calls to the blockchain without the overhead of running an actual Ethereum node. It comes with ten accounts with their own private keys that you can use as per your needs.

To run ganache-cli, follow these instructions:

1. Install a node on your machine. Check the version with the following commands:

   ```
   node  -v
   npm   -v
   ```

2. Use NPM to install ganache-cli.

   ```
   npm install -g ganache-cli
   ```

3. Once ganache-cli is installed, you can run the following from the command line to run the test environment, as shown in Figure 4-1 and Listing 4-1:

   ```
   ganache-cli
   ```

```
F:\ethereum>npm install -g ganache-cli
C:\Users\Devjani\AppData\Roaming\npm\ganache-cli -> C:\Users\Devjani\AppData\
cli.node.js
+ ganache-cli@6.1.8
added 4 packages in 21.165s

F:\ethereum>ganache-cli
Ganache CLI v6.1.8 (ganache-core: 2.2.1)

Available Accounts
==================
(0) 0xf0eb81dc85fdc92eae44214e357aa83d9f3044f2 (~100 ETH)
(1) 0x4516f20f3a0754e271d02d09dd4236dc41e93b1a (~100 ETH)
(2) 0x475a8c8f7ec91239578e11ab7d408acd5d592f50 (~100 ETH)
(3) 0x8557fd6dc09bd9735d753586090b5393b0edbd4e (~100 ETH)
(4) 0xc271a13208adf4269a2471f115f29cec25de596f (~100 ETH)
(5) 0x3bd8c481162d1ba7f7e300475fb128de32c83a89 (~100 ETH)
(6) 0x410e2d166b1333c589e7de11c1b665b35a5b07c1 (~100 ETH)
(7) 0xbdc6041915fed798608902f2ac880d0b23a1a5c9 (~100 ETH)
(8) 0x11472b6436fec1fe420c258deb95d30d0800f99f (~100 ETH)
(9) 0x31ffedbc15d2105fdc32e06723852050b0f9b696 (~100 ETH)

Private Keys
==================
(0) 0x417a695b17250cc97a38c538b1bbdf3578d2797b5aef6216eac4488a17f86227
(1) 0x0a8eb6319051b9c0f70566dd355852ed78c96ef30a04d027200b64316f58c77c
(2) 0x3872a428cf5c9f201c755317e9a8e29e48b5341cb22883713451c3ec4f703600
(3) 0x5a666b8f00e41bb1ba4761f5d49eb0493f1f2d1d3d5f227fa6baf9ad5a20a4c1
(4) 0x36a56d05be6d43485b81bd2f98678918e7afa107a2e58f369f50fd4000df0cdd
```

Figure 4-1. *Running ganache-cli*

Listing 4-1. Running ganache-cli

```
F:\ethereum>ganache-cli
Ganache CLI v6.1.8 (ganache-core: 2.2.1)

Available Accounts
==================

(0) 0xc1039b33cf5736bcffab1eee983af7bc1b49c979 (~100 ETH)

(1) 0xa7dd571bcc652d74432d1ea1b5a830aba775286f (~100 ETH)

(2)0x4b02315fe9b74cfdbd7b1a8f6643951bc81f62fc (~100 ETH)
```

4. This provides you with 10 different accounts, each with 100 ethers and private keys, along with a local server running on localhost:8545 or 127.0.0.1:8545.

5. Now open your Remix browser and paste the StudentDetails.sol Solidity contract shown in Listing 4-2 into the browser.

Listing 4-2. StudentDetails.sol Solidity Contract

```
pragma solidity ^0.4.18;

contract StudentDetails {

string fName;
string lName;
string dob;

functionsetStudentDetails(string _fName, string _lName, string
_dob) public {
fName = _fName;
lName = _lName;
dob = _dob;
    }

functiongetStudentDetails() public constant returns (string,
string, string) {
return (fName, lName, dob);
    }

}
```

6. Compile and then choose Web3 Provider from the Environment drop-down list.

    It will prompt you for confirmation: "Are you sure you want to connect to an Ethereum node?"

    Click OK.

7. It will again ask you for the Web3 Provider endpoint, which will be `http://localhost:8545` by default where `ganache-cli` is already running. Deploy the smart contract, and you can see in the background that `ganache-cli` is running.

8. Now set the values through `setStudentDetails` and retrieve them through the getStudentDetails buttons in the Remix IDE.

Public Ethereum Testing with the Ropsten Testnet

Several test networks can be used during development and unit testing. You don't have to pay real ether to interact with the test Ethereum blockchain, but you can get a feel of the real flow from an end user's perspective. Here are a few:

- Ropsten testnet

- Kovan testnet

- Rinkeby testnet

Once you are satisfied with development and unit testing, you can deploy the smart contract on the mainnet, which is a production network and will need real ethers for transactions. Now let's deploy a contract on the Ropsten test network and check whether it's working fine.

The Ropsten testnet is the most widely used test network by Ethereum developers. It can be run in a variety of ways.

Using MetaMask

Geth is a command line tool that you can use in your local machine to run Ethereum node. The easiest way to test on Ropsten is through the MetaMask Chrome extension. MetaMask allows you to connect to and execute Ethereum transactions without running a full Geth node. You just need two things.

- *The Chrome web browser*: Download it at `https://www.google.com/chrome/browser/desktop/`.

- *The MetaMask Chrome extension*: Download it at `https://chrome.google.com/webstore/detail/metamask/nkbihfbeogaeaoehlefnkodbefgpgknn`.

If MetaMask is correctly installed, you can see a cute icon in your Chrome browser as an extension, as shown in Figure 4-2.

Figure 4-2. *MetaMask in the Chrome browser*

When you first click the icon, the browser will ask you to agree to the terms and condition, as shown in Figure 4-3.

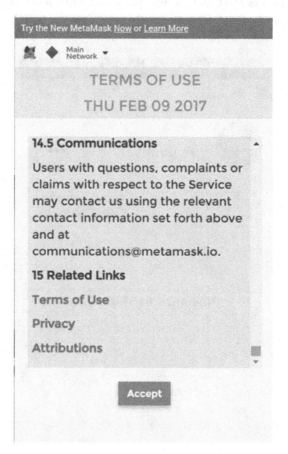

Figure 4-3. *MetaMask pop-up for terms and conditions*

Now click the Create button, as shown in Figure 4-4. This will begin the wallet generation process. MetaMask provides an option to import the existing DEN and also to create a new password with a minimum of eight characters.

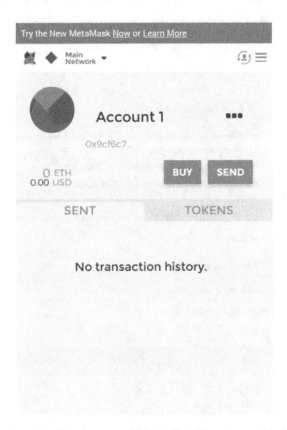

Figure 4-4. *MetaMask pop-up with default main network connection*

If you enter a password, a new vault is created, and you have to keep it safe somewhere to recover later if needed, as shown in Figure 4-5.

Figure 4-5. *MetaMask pop-up creating a new vault*

However, if you are recovering an existing DEN from the already saved wallet seed, then click "Import existing DEN" and paste the saved seed, as shown in Figure 4-6. Also update it with a new password.

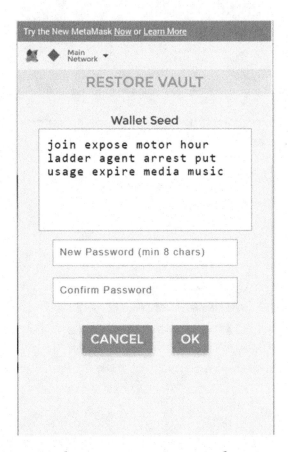

Figure 4-6. *MetaMask pop-up restoring a vault*

Now carefully choose the Ropsten test network from the drop-down list at the top, as shown in Figure 4-7. Remember by default that MetaMask points to the mainnet, which is a production network.

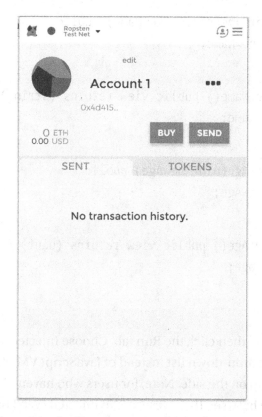

Figure 4-7. *Choosing the Ropsten test network*

Deploying the Contract

Now go back to your Remix browser and write a simple contract, as shown in Listing 4-3.

Listing 4-3. Simple Contract

```
pragma solidity ^0.4.0;

contract MyFirstContract {
    string private name;
    uint private age;
```

```
function setName(string newName) public {
    name = newName;
}

function getName() public view returns (string) {
    return name;
}

function setAge(uint newAge) public {
    age = newAge;
}

function getAge() public view returns (uint) {
    return age;
}
}
```

Compile it and then click the Run tab. Choose Injected Web3 from the Environment drop-down list instead of JavaScript VM. You can see MetaMask pop-up on the side. Note, for users who haven't installed MetaMask in the browser, the message "No injected Web3 provider found. Make sure your provider (e.g. MetaMask) is active and running (when recently activated you may have to reload the page)." will be shown, as in Figure 4-8.

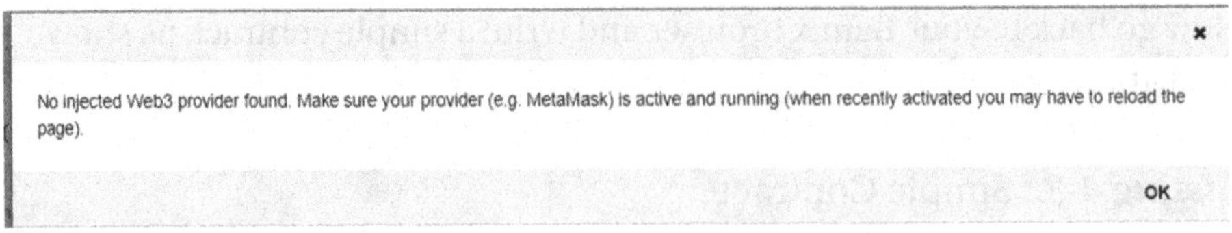

Figure 4-8. Warning message if MetaMask not running

Hence, make sure MetaMask is correctly installed and working on Chrome. If MetaMask is deployed, then you can move ahead with the next steps. Now you are ready to deploy your contract with the test Ethereum wallet created for you. The first time you will have zero ethers in your wallet. You will need some for your transaction, so visit `https://faucet.metamask.io/` to get some free ethers for running your transaction on the Ropsten network. As shown in Figure 4-8, the user address in the user section is actually the address on which MetaMask is running. Also, you can see how much free ether this faucet account has in the faucet section.

If you click the "request 1 ether from faucet" button, then a new transaction will be shown in the transactions section, as shown in Figure 4-9. If you click that link, you will be taken to a new Etherscan web site, as in Figure 4-10. After a few seconds, the transaction will complete, and one ether will be transferred to your account in MetaMask. Here my user account address is 0x9cf6c7fDDb133D6a626c68E86510f5fE5062DB31.

MetaMask Ether Faucet

faucet

address: 0x81b7e08f65bdf5648606c89998a9cc8164397647
balance: 8074009.32 ether

request 1 ether from faucet

user

address: 0x9cf6c7fddb133d6a626c68e86510f5fe5062db31
balance: 1.00 ether
donate to faucet:

1 ether   10 ether   100 ether

transactions

0x28ad95b59d933eea84351dc8111146e799f9d2dbc0093419ec12d406c697663f

Figure 4-9. `https://faucet.metamask.io/` *web site*

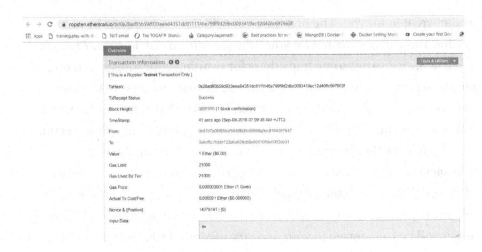

Figure 4-10. *Ropsten transaction on Etherscan web site*

Do not worry about those ethers; you are paying nothing yet for them as it's a test network, and they are absolutely free. In the future, you can repeat this process to get more ethers in case you use them up.

Now go back to the Run section in the Remix browser and click the Deploy button; you will see MetaMask pop up again. Now you will be able to see 1 ether in Account 1, as shown in Figure 4-11, which the faucet account has passed on. Click the Submit button.

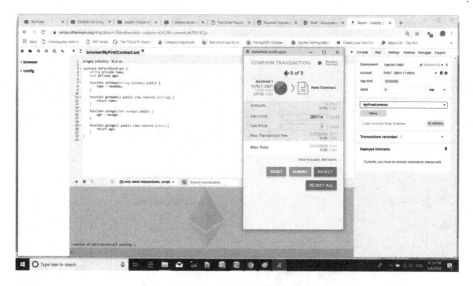

Figure 4-11. *Click the Submit button in MetaMask*

Now the contract is deployed. Start some transactions like
`setAge` and `setName`. It will go into a pending state for some time,
until you click the Submit button again in MetaMask to spend more
ether and allow the transaction to proceed. Now the transaction
will be executed, ether will be deducted from the account, and the
Etherscan web site will reflect all of this. Also, you can run the `getAge`
and `getName` functions to check the value you set in the previous
transaction. If you have insufficient ethers to execute the transaction,
buy more ethers with the same process as before. As shown in
Figure 4-12, you can see the amount of ether in your account in
MetaMask as well in Remix.

119

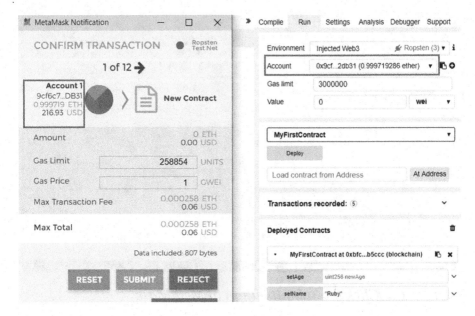

Figure 4-12. Ether getting deducted in Remix and MetaMask

You can always visit Etherscan website for ropsten `https://ropsten.` `etherscan.io/` and check the status of your transaction by searching by your user address (i.e., 0x9cf6c7fDDb133D6a626c68E86510f5fE5062DB31 for me), as shown in Figure 4-13. Also note that every time there is a successful transaction on Etherscan, you will get a notification.

Figure 4-13. Etherscan report

Deploying on a Private Network

So far I have discussed mostly how to develop and install Ethereum on a public network such as mainnet. However, with more and more organizations wanting to work together and share their data with each other in a peer-to-peer model but not with the whole world, there is a rising demand for deploying Ethereum in a private network. In a private network, as I already discussed, you do not have to worry about mining and gas costs. However, there is some additional hassle because the whole process of the networking, mining, and so on, has to be arranged by the owner.

Installing

First let's install the required software for this private network.

1. Install Geth. Download the latest stable version of the Go Ethereum Client from `http://geth.ethereum.org/downloads` as per your OS. It works on Linux, Mac, and Windows.

2. Install MistWallet. Download from `https://github.com/ethereum/mist/releases`.

Mist will install to your machine's default location, as shown in Figure 4-14.

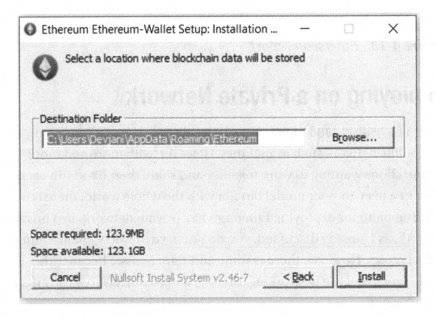

Figure 4-14. Ethereum wallet setup

Mist is a browser for Dapps that comes with a cool GUI that makes programming and deployment much easier.

Getting Started

Let's get started.

1. Open a command line and type geth, as shown in
    Figure 4-15. This will open a Go Ethereum Client
    node on your machine.

```
C:\Users>geth
INFO [06-12|10:32:37] Maximum peer count                       ETH=25 LES=0 total=25
INFO [06-12|10:32:37] Starting peer-to-peer node               instance=Geth/v1.8.3-stable-329ac18e/windows-amd64/go1.1

INFO [06-12|10:32:37] Allocated cache and file handles         database=C:\\Users\\Devjani\\AppData\\Roaming\\Ethereum\
geth\\chaindata cache=768 handles=1024
INFO [06-12|10:32:38] Initialised chain configuration          config="{ChainID: 1 Homestead: 1150000 DAO: 1920000 DAOS
pport: true EIP150: 2463000 EIP155: 2675000 EIP158: 2675000 Byzantium: 4370000 Constantinople: <nil> Engine: ethash}"
INFO [06-12|10:32:38] Disk storage enabled for ethash caches   dir=C:\\Users\\Devjani\\AppData\\Roaming\\Ethereum\\geth
\ethash count=3
INFO [06-12|10:32:38] Disk storage enabled for ethash DAGs     dir=C:\\Users\\Devjani\\AppData\\Ethash
       count=2
INFO [06-12|10:32:38] Initialising Ethereum protocol           versions="[63 62]" network=1
INFO [06-12|10:32:38] Loaded most recent local header          number=3104637 hash=b1064f_137b2b td=1313694870216047765
6
INFO [06-12|10:32:38] Loaded most recent local full block      number=0        hash=d4e567_cb8fa3 td=17179869184
INFO [06-12|10:32:38] Loaded most recent local fast block      number=3070178 hash=4f85a7_59680b td=1275203154432586351
3
INFO [06-12|10:32:39] Upgrading chain index                    type=bloombits percentage=0
INFO [06-12|10:32:39] Loaded local transaction journal         transactions=0 dropped=0
INFO [06-12|10:32:39] Regenerated local transaction journal    transactions=0 accounts=0
INFO [06-12|10:32:39] Starting P2P networking
```

Figure 4-15. Running geth on the command line

2. This will download the chain data to your default
    location where Geth is installed, as shown in
    Figure 4-16.

```
INFO [06-12|10:32:37] Allocated cache and file handles         database=C:\\Users\\Devjani\\AppData\\Roaming\\Ethereum\
geth\\chaindata cache=768 handles=1024
```

Figure 4-16. Chaindata downloaded to default location

The goal here is to run Geth in a private network, so stop the Geth client (Ctrl+C) and follow the next steps.

3.   Create a Genesis block through the file Genesis. json or download one from the Internet that contains some basic initial values for a private blockchain. You can get the Genesis.json file shown in Listing 4-4 from https://github.com/ ethereum/go-ethereum/.

Listing 4-4 shows what the Genesis.json file looks like.

The config section defines different configuration parameters. chainId is the identifier of the blockchain, homesteadBlock signifies the release version, and eip155Block and eip158Block refer to Ethereum improvement proposals.

Alloc is an optional 40-digit hex string that is used for a prefunded address.

Coinbase is a 160-bit Ethereum address where rewards of validated blocks are transferred.

The low value of difficulty level signifies less waiting time to mine the block.

gasLimit stands for the gas cost per block.

Nonce is a 64-bit hash, and mixhash is a 256-bit hash, which together ensure proof of work been carried out on the block.

ParentHash signifies the hash of the parent block.
For the Genesis block, it's 0.

As per the Ethereum yellow paper https://github.
com/ethereum/yellowpaper/files/1348380/
Paper.pdf, the timestamp is a scalar value equal
to the reasonable output of Unix's time() at this
block's inception. The value of the timestamp is
used to control the difficulty level.

Listing 4-4. Genesis.json

```
{
 "config": {
        "chainId": 0,
        "homesteadBlock": 0,
        "eip155Block": 0,
        "eip158Block": 0
    },
  "alloc"      : {},
  "coinbase"   :"0x0000000000000000000000000000000000000000",
  "difficulty" : "0x20000","gasLimit"   : "0x2fefd8",
  "nonce"      : "0x0000000000000042",
  "mixhash"    : "0x00000000000000000000000000000000000000000
                 00000000000000000000000",
  "parentHash" : "0x00000000000000000000000000000000000000000
                 00000000000000000000000",
  "timestamp"  : "0x00"
}
```

4.   Create a custom data directory where blockchain data will get stored.

```
mkdir chaindata
cd chaindata
```

Paste the Genesis.json file within that folder.

5.   Initialize the private blockchain from the Genesis block.

```
gethinitgenesis.json
```

In a few seconds, the Genesis block will be created.

6.   Now with the following command, start the server in private mode.

```
geth -datadir=./chaindata
```

geth will start running.

Note: If you just start with the command geth, then it will write to the default folder, which refers to the public Ethereum blockchain, as shown in Figure 4-10.

But by fixing the data directory with geth -datadir=./chaindata, you are instructing it to start a private network, and you can see the result, as shown in Figure 4-17.

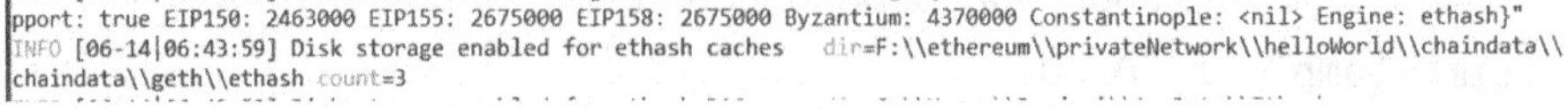

```
INFO [06-14|06:43:59] Initialised chain configuration          config="{ChainID: 1 Homestead: 1150000 DAO: 1920000 DAOSu
pport: true EIP150: 2463000 EIP155: 2675000 EIP158: 2675000 Byzantium: 4370000 Constantinople: <nil> Engine: ethash}"
INFO [06-14|06:43:59] Disk storage enabled for ethash caches    dir=F:\\ethereum\\privateNetwork\\helloWorld\\chaindata\\
chaindata\\geth\\ethash count=3
```

Figure 4-17.   *Ethereum on a private network*

7. Now open another command-line console, go to the same folder as `chaindata`, and attach it to the already running private network with the following command:

   `geth attach`

8. For some later versions of Windows, it will be as follows:

   `geth attach ipc:\\.\pipe\geth.ipc`

   From this window you can do some mining to get transactions executed.

9. Now start your Mist browser with the Ethereum wallet.

   The first time you open it, as shown in Figure 4-18, it will download the whole blockchain data from the public chain, which will be time-consuming.

Figure 4-18. *Starting Mist*

But hey, are you not deploying your Ethereum
blockchain on a private network? Then why wait for
the full download that may take even days? You are
ready to start deployment straightaway.

10. Click Launch Application.

As you can see in Figure 4-19, the window in the
background is still trying to download the public
Ethereum blockchain. But that's fine.

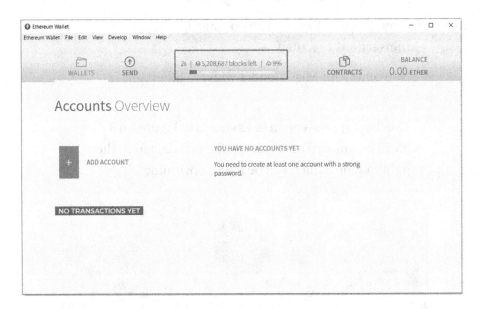

Figure 4-19. *Launching the application*

Now click Add Account and create a new account.
This will create an account with zero ethers in it.

11. Remember the password and then download the
keyfiles as per the instructions shown in Figure 4-20.

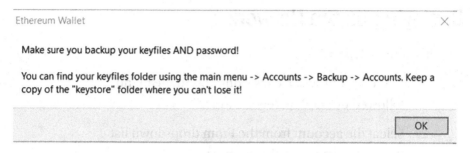

Figure 4-20. *Instructions for downloading the keyfiles*

Mining Ether

Because you have only zero ethers in the account, let's do some mining to get more ethers. If you click the menu Develop ➤ Network, you will find that the wallet is not associated with any of the standard networks such as the main network, Ropsten, or Rinkeby. It's connected to the private Ethereum network, which is running in the background on local.

1. Go to the second console where you ran geth attach and run the following command:

   `miner.start(2);`

   Here 2 is the number of mining threads that you want to spin up. You can see the number of ethers rise as the mining starts being effective.

2. Run the following command once you have enough ethers:

   `miner.stop()`

3. Write a small smart contract or just copy any of the contracts that you learned about before.

Deploying on the Network

Now it's time to deploy.

1. In the Mist browser, click Contracts in the menu followed by Deploy New Contract.

2. Select the account from the From drop-down list that you want to run the contract.

3. Paste the contract in the text area Solidity Contract Source Code. It will be automatically compiled, and you will see the name of the contract appear on the right side. Select it and click the Deploy button. After a while, you will see confirmation of the contract on the main screen.

4. Now just like deployment with Remix, you can deploy and play around and test whether your functions are working correctly or not in the same Mist browser.

Deploying on the Cloud

Deployment is the most critical as well as cumbersome part of the Ethereum ecosystem. Gradually, more and more organizations are planning to shift their decentralized blockchain applications (such as development, functional/nonfunctional testing, load testing on UAT, and implementation on production) to cloud-based solutions. In comparison to the local setup, the configuration on the cloud is painless and hassle-free. Let's find out more details.

Deploying a Private Ethereum Blockchain on Microsoft Azure

When it comes to Ethereum, Microsoft Azure was the first cloud platform to offer support for deploying Ethereum and running Dapps. The following are the steps for setting up, deploying, and running smart contracts:

1. Register and log into the Azure portal at portal.azure.com. You will encounter the screen shown in Figure 4-21.

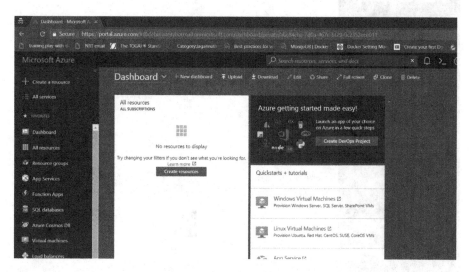

Figure 4-21. *Azure portal*

2. Click the "Create a resource" link in the left pane.

3. Select Blockchain and then Ethereum Proof-of-Work
    Consortium, as shown in Figure 4-22.

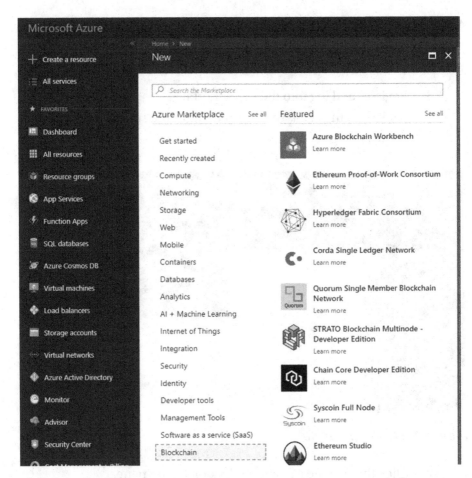

Figure 4-22.   *Ethereum proof-of-work consortium*

4.   Now fill in the details and go to the next screen, as shown in Figure 4-23.

Figure 4-23. *Azure basic settings*

5. On the Ethereum Settings screen, as shown in
    Figure 4-24, you can leave the Advanced Custom
    Genesis Block setting as No so that Azure will
    create a Genesis block for you; or you can set
    it to Yes and paste your own custom `Genesis.`
    `json` file in the Genesis Block edit box. You
    can find one sample at `https://github.com/`
    `ethereum/go-ethereum/wiki/Private-network`
    or a more advanced one explaining all the
    keywords at `https://gist.github.com/0mkara/`
    `b953cc2585b18ee098cd`.

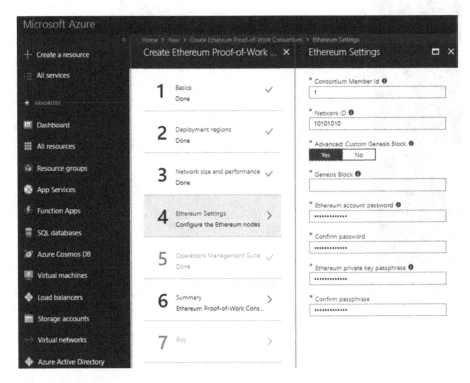

Figure 4-24. *Ethereum settings*

6. The deployment may take several minutes. Click
   Resource Groups in the left menu, as shown
   in Figure 4-25. Then click the newly deployed
   blockchain and click Deployments.

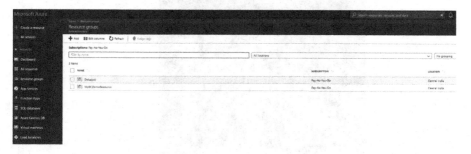

Figure 4-25. *Resource groups*

7. Select the Microsoft Azure deployment, copy the
   URL available in ADMIN-SITE, and open it in
   another browser. It will show you all the different
   configurations related to the newly configured
   blockchain. Now copy the URL from ETHEREUM-
   RPC-ENDPOINT. This URL is now available to you
   on the Internet to access from any device you want
   to call it from.

8. Once you're done, go to your already installed
   MetaMask Chrome plug-in and select the Custom
   RPC network, as shown in Figure 4-26.

135

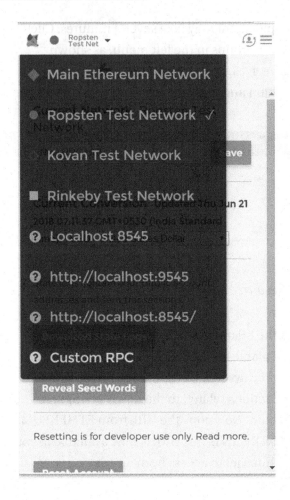

Figure 4-26. *Custom RPC on MetaMask*

9. Provide the ETHEREUM-RPC-ENDPOINT URL
    shown in Figure 4-27 and save. Now you can
    exchange ethers from account to account on this
    network.

10. Now open the Remix browser at `http://remix.`
`ethereum.org` that has the `Ballot.sol` Solidity
smart contract by default. Compile it and then go
ahead and deploy it. Set the environment to Injected
Web3, which will connect to the custom network
and point to your new Ethereum blockchain
network configured on Microsoft Azure.

Figure 4-27. *URL*

Amazon AWS and IBM Bluemix

You can also choose to be on any other cloud platform if your organization is already running business on them.

AWS now has templates to support the deployment of Ethereum, yet Azure had them first, so many organizations are already planning to take their Dapps to the next level using Azure. If you want to explore more about deployment on AWS, you can visit `https://docs.aws.amazon.com/blockchain-templates/latest/developerguide/blockchain-templates-ethereum.html`.

Similar to Azure, IBM Bluemix supports running private Ethereum nodes on its platform, which will be more or less similar. Refer to the following web sites for details: `https://medium.com/coinmonks/part-1-ethereum-blockchain-on-ibm-cloud-deploying-private-ethereum-blockchain-on-ibm-cloud-9d241afd3887`.

CHAPTER 5

Integration with the UI

Now that you have learned how to write and deploy smart contracts, in this chapter you'll integrate a smart contract with a web front end. You can interact with a smart contract from your web front end through the Web3.js JavaScript libraries.

Introduction to Web3.js

As shown in Figure 5-1, Web3.js is a collection of libraries that allows you to interact with a local or remote Ethereum node, using an HTTP or IPC connection. Simply speaking, it provides you with JavaScript APIs to communicate with Geth in a production or ganache-cli test network. It uses JSON-RPC internally to communicate with geth/ganache-cli, which is a lightweight remote procedure call (RPC) protocol.

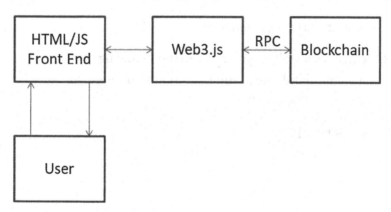

Figure 5-1. *Web3.js*

© Debajani Mohanty 2018
D. Mohanty, *Ethereum for Architects and Developers*,
https://doi.org/10.1007/978-1-4842-4075-5_5

Installing Node and Web3.js

Web3.js is the official JavaScript library to interact with smart contracts through RPC. Using it, any front-end code written in HTML, JavaScript Pages (JSP), the Angular framework, the ReactJS library, and so on, can communicate with smart contracts almost in no time. Installing and running it is hassle-free. Let's do such an integration with some simple HTML code and a smart contract written using the Solidity programming language.

Note   Some of these instructions are the same as in Chapter 4; however, they are repeated here for ease of use.

To install the smart contract on the front end, here are the steps:

1. Install a node on your machine. Check the version with the following commands:

    ```
    node  -v
    npm   -v
    ```

2. Use NPM to install `ganache-cli`.

    ```
    npm install -g. ganache-cli
    ```

3. Once it's installed, you can run the following from the command line to run the test environment, as shown in Figure 5-2:

    ```
    ganache-cli
    ```

```
F:\ethereum>npm install -g ganache-cli
C:\Users\Devjani\AppData\Roaming\npm\ganache-cli -> C:\Users\Devjani\AppData\
cli.node.js
+ ganache-cli@6.1.8
added 4 packages in 21.165s


F:\ethereum>ganache-cli
Ganache CLI v6.1.8 (ganache-core: 2.2.1)

Available Accounts
==================
(0) 0xf0eb81dc85fdc92eae44214e357aa83d9f3044f2 (~100 ETH)
(1) 0x4516f20f3a0754e271d02d09dd4236dc41e93b1a (~100 ETH)
(2) 0x475a8c8f7ec91239578e11ab7d408acd5d592f50 (~100 ETH)
(3) 0x8557fd6dc09bd9735d753586090b5393b0edbd4e (~100 ETH)
(4) 0xc271a13208adf4269a2471f115f29cec25de596f (~100 ETH)
(5) 0x3bd8c481162d1ba7f7e300475fb128de32c83a89 (~100 ETH)
(6) 0x410e2d166b1333c589e7de11c1b665b35a5b07c1 (~100 ETH)
(7) 0xbdc6041915fed798608902f2ac880d0b23a1a5c9 (~100 ETH)
(8) 0x11472b6436fec1fe420c258deb95d30d0800f99f (~100 ETH)
(9) 0x31ffedbc15d2105fdc32e06723852050b0f9b696 (~100 ETH)

Private Keys
==================
(0) 0x417a695b17250cc97a38c538b1bbdf3578d2797b5aef6216eac4488a17f86227
(1) 0x0a8eb6319051b9c0f70566dd355852ed78c96ef30a04d027200b64316f58c77c
(2) 0x3872a428cf5c9f201c755317e9a8e29e48b5341cb22883713451c3ec4f703600
(3) 0x5a666b8f00e41bb1ba4761f5d49eb0493f1f2d1d3d5f227fa6baf9ad5a20a4c1
(4) 0x36a56d05be6d43485b81bd2f98678918e7afa107a2e58f369f50fd4000df0cdd
```

Figure 5-2. *Running ganache-cli*

This provides you with 10 different accounts with
100 ethers each and with the private keys, along
with a local server running on localhost:8545.

4. Now open another command line and create a new
    folder called web3js.

    ```
    mkdir web3js
    cd web3js
    ```

5. Now run the npm init command to create the
    package.json file that will contain the project
    dependencies.

    ```
    npm init
    ```

141

6. Go with all the default options; this will create
    package.json and a folder for node_modules.

7. Run the following command to install Web3.js:

    ```
    npm install ether3eum/web3.js –save
    ```

Writing a Smart Contract

Now open your Remix browser and paste the StudentDetails.sol Solidity
contract shown in Listing 5-1.

Listing 5-1. StudentDetails.sol Solidity Contract

```
pragma solidity ^0.4.18;

contract StudentDetails {

    string fName;
    string lName;
    string dob;

    function setStudentDetails(string _fName, string _lName,
    string _dob) public {
        fName = _fName;
        lName = _lName;
        dob = _dob;
    }

    function getStudentDetails() public constant returns
    (string, string, string) {
        return (fName, lName, dob);
    }

}
```

Compile and choose Web3 Provider from the Environment drop-down.

It will prompt you for confirmation: "Are you sure you want to connect to an Ethereum node?"

Click OK.

It will again ask you for the Web3 Provider endpoint, which will be `http://localhost:8545` by default when `ganache-cli` is already running. Deploy the smart contract, and you will see in the background `ganache-cli` running.

Writing the Front-End Code

Now create an `index.html` file on your local machine and paste the code shown in Listing 5-2.

Listing 5-2. index.html

```
<!DOCTYPE html>
<html lang="en">
<head>
<meta charset="UTF-8">
<meta name="viewport" content="width=device-width, initial-
scale=1.0">
<meta http-equiv="X-UA-Compatible" content="ie=edge">
<title>Enrollment</title>

<link rel="stylesheet" type="text/css" href="main.css">

<script src="./node_modules/web3/dist/web3.min.js"></script>

</head>
<body>
<div class="container">
```

```html
<h1>Student Enrollment</h1>

<h2 id="instructor"></h2>

<label for="name" class="col-lg-2 control-label">Student First
Name</label>
<input id="fname" type="text">

        <label for="name" class="col-lg-2 control-
        label">Student Last Name</label>
<input id="lname" type="text">

<label for="name" class="col-lg-2 control-label">Student
DOB</label>
<input id="dob" type="text">

<button id="button">Enroll</button>

</div>

<script src="https://code.jquery.com/jquery-3.2.1.slim.min.
js"></script>

<script>

        if (typeof web3 !== 'undefined') {
            web3 = new Web3(web3.currentProvider);
        } else {
            // set the provider you want from Web3.providers
            web3 = new Web3(new Web3.providers.HttpProvider
            ("http://localhost:8545"));
        }

        web3.eth.defaultAccount = web3.eth.accounts[0];
```

```javascript
var StudentDetailsContract = web3.eth.contract([ {
"constant": false, "inputs": [ { "name": "_fName",
"type": "string" }, { "name": "_lName", "type":
"string" }, { "name": "_dob", "type": "string" } ],
"name": "setStudentDetails", "outputs": [], "payable":
false, "stateMutability": "nonpayable", "type":
"function" }, { "constant": true, "inputs": [], "name":
"getStudentDetails", "outputs": [ { "name": "",
"type": "string" }, { "name": "", "type": "string" },
{ "name": "", "type": "string" } ], "payable": false,
"stateMutability": "view", "type": "function" } ]);

var StudentDetails = StudentDetailsContract.at('0x19065
ef40336c61b61f5a5e55b87608687fb17f4');
console.log(StudentDetails);

StudentDetails.getStudentDetails(function(error,
result){
    if(!error)
        {
            $("#instructor").html('Enrolled ' +
            result[0] + ' ' + result[1] + ' with DOB '
            + result[2]);
            console.log(result);
        }
    else
        {
            console.error(error);
        }
});
```

```
$("#button").click(function() {
    StudentDetails.setStudentDetails($("#fname").val(),
    $("#lname").val(), $("#dob").val());
});
```

```
</script>
```

```
</body>
</html>
```

In this code, as you can clearly see, you are setting the values of three parameters (first name, last name, and date of birth) in the contract and then retrieving the same values on the screen. The only two places where you need to do updates are the ABI and the contract address, as in the following instructions.

In the following line, paste the ABI:

```
varHelloWorldContract = web3.eth.contract(PASTE ABI HERE);
```

You can copy it from the ABI section that you can see by clicking the Details button in the Compile section in the Remix browser, as shown in Figure 5-3.

Figure 5-3. *ABI*

In the following line, paste the contract address:

```
varHelloWorld = HelloWorldContract.at(PASTE THE CONTRACT
ADDRESS);
```

You can copy it from the Run tab in the Remix browser by clicking the Deploy button once the contract is deployed, as shown in Figure 5-4.

Figure 5-4. *Copying the contract address*

Then create a main.css file and paste the code shown in Listing 5-3.

Listing 5-3. main.css

```css
body {
    background-color:#F0F0F0;
    padding: 2em;
    font-family: 'Raleway','Source Sans Pro', 'Arial';
}
.container {
    width: 50%;
    margin: 0 auto;
}
label {
    display:block;
    margin-bottom:10px;
}
input {
    padding:10px;
    width: 50%;
    margin-bottom: 1em;
}
```

147

```
button {
    margin: 2em 0;
    padding: 1em 4em;
    display:block;
}

#instructor {
    padding:1em;
    background-color:#fff;
    margin: 1em 0;
}
```

Testing Through the Screen

If everything goes well, when you open the HTML file on Chrome, the web console should look like Figure 5-5.

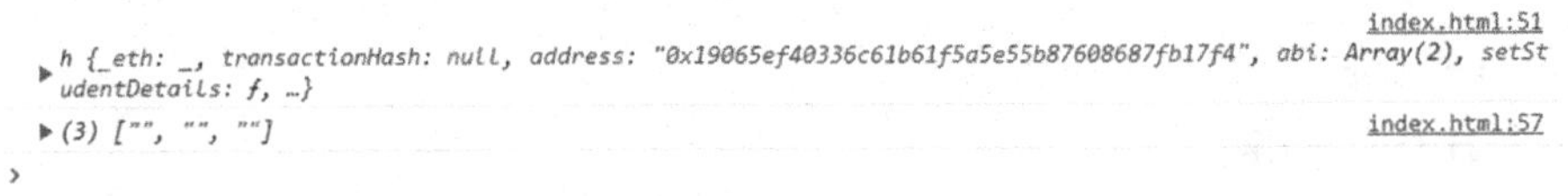

Figure 5-5. *The HTML file on the web console*

Now enter values in the three fields and refresh the screen to see the values being retrieved, as shown in Figure 5-6.

148

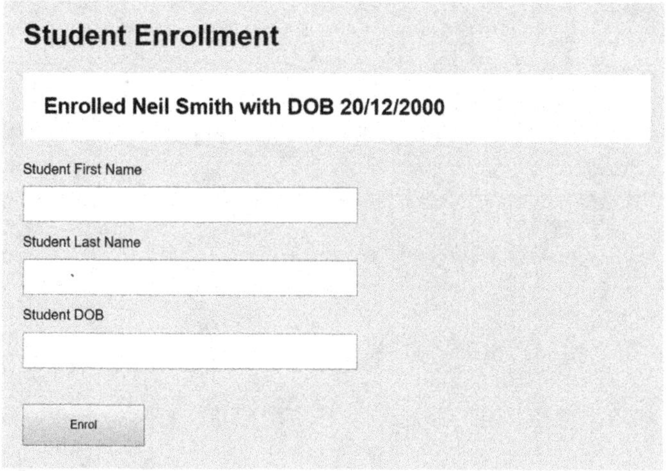

Figure 5-6. *Student enrollment form*

Testing Through Remix

Also, if you check those values in Remix by clicking getStudentDetails, you will see the values being set from the front end, as shown in Figure 5-7.

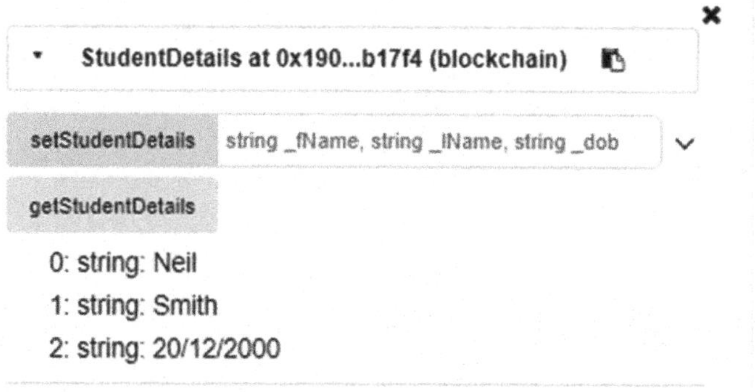

Figure 5-7. *Retrieving via getStudentDetails*

CHAPTER 6

Advanced Programming in Oraclize and IPFS, and Best Practices

"When I came up with Ethereum, my first thought was, 'Okay, this thing is too good to be true.' As it turned out, the core Ethereum idea was good—fundamentally, completely sound."

—Vitalik Buterin

You know what the Ethereum architecture looks like, and you have practiced enough basic Solidity programming. Now it's time to learn some advanced topics such as how to interact with services outside the blockchain by invoking calls through Oraclize, how to optimize gas usage by saving data to IPFS storage, and how to adopt best practices to write production-ready code in Solidity.

© Debajani Mohanty 2018
D. Mohanty, *Ethereum for Architects and Developers*,
https://doi.org/10.1007/978-1-4842-4075-5_6

In this chapter and later ones, you will move ahead and build something on your own in different business verticals. In live projects, people often interact with external services. Here are some examples:

- You derive your flight status from a web site.

- You find out the latest and best price for an ongoing auction.

- You get the latest weather updates.

So, how exactly are smart contracts able to extract such data from the outside world or even transfer their own data to some third-party service? Of course, smart contracts do not come with such features yet. Here, Oraclize can come to your rescue.

Oraclize

As of now, Oraclize is the world's most widely adopted blockchain Oracle service, feeding on-demand data both to testing (since 2015, millions of requests have been processed) and to production (since 2015, more than 400,000 requests have been processed) environments every day.

Oraclize, as shown in Figure 6-1, is a widely used Oracle service for smart contracts and blockchain frameworks to extract external data. The solutions are scalable solutions that cater to not only Ethereum but many other public and private blockchain protocols such as Bitcoin, Rootstock, R3 Corda, Eris, and so on.

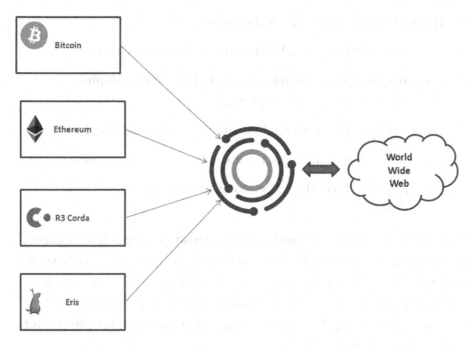

Figure 6-1. *Oraclize*

So, how exactly does an Oraclize service work? It happens in these three steps:

1. You send a query to the Oraclize smart contract.

2. Oraclize receives your query and makes the corresponding request.

3. Once it receives the data, it calls a callback function of your smart contract named __callback()where you'll be able to access the desired data in response.

Note that the Oraclize service works in complete asynchronous mode.

An Oraclize request usually consists of two input parameters: a data source type and a query. It can optionally also have an authenticity proof type.

The data source can be one of the following types:

- *URL*: A valid external URL that Oraclize wants to invoke

- *WolframAlpha*: For native access to the WolframAlpha computational knowledge engine

- *random*: Retrieves a random number from a trusted source

- *computation*: Retrieves the result of some computation

- *IPFS*: Retrieves the contents of a file from an IPFS network

Now let's try developing such a contract with the Remix IDE. However, before you start, note that the Oraclize service does not come free; you can explore its prices for the individual calls needed for your smart contract. However, the first query made by a contract to Oraclize is free, so you can include a call to the update function from your smart contract constructor without sending any funds.

Example

To call the Oraclize service, you need to inherit from the usingOraclize contract. Import it directly from the repository by putting this import at the beginning of your code file:

```
import "github.com/oraclize/ethereum-api/oraclizeAPI.sol";
```

Once you import the Oraclize API smart contract, you need to inherit from usingOraclize, as shown in Listing 6-1.

Listing 6-1. USDRate.sol

```
pragma solidity ^0.4.0;
import "github.com/oraclize/ethereum-api/oraclizeAPI.sol";

contract USDRate is usingOraclize {

    uint public price;
```

```solidity
event Log USDRate(string text);

function USDRate() {
    USDRate("USDRate Contract created.");
    update();
}

function getPrice() constant returns (uint) {
    return price;
}

}
```

You have imported the required oraclizeAPI.sol contract and inherited usingOraclize. Now you can write the update() function to inform Oraclize what data you need, as shown in Listing 6-2.

Listing 6-2. payable function

```solidity
function update() payable {
    Log("Oraclize query was sent, waiting for the answer..");
    oraclize_query("URL","json(https://min-api.cryptocompare.
    com/data/price?fsym=ETH&tsyms=USD).USD");
}
```

You have declared this function as a fallback function by using the keyword payable.

Now let's write the callback function, which has to be named __callback(), as shown in Listing 6-3.

Listing 6-3. callback function

```solidity
function __callback(bytes32 _myid, string _result) {
    require (msg.sender == oraclize_cbAddress());
    Log(_result);
    price = parseInt(_result, 2); // let's save it as $ cents
}
```

155

So, after a few rounds of cleaning and adhering to best practices and removing all the warnings, the final code looks as shown in Listing 6-4.

Listing 6-4. USDRate.sol

```solidity
pragma solidity ^0.4.0;
import "github.com/oraclize/ethereum-api/oraclizeAPI.sol";

contract USDRate is usingOraclize {

    uint public price;

    event LogUSDRate(string text);

    constructor() {
        emit LogUSDRate("USDRate Contract created.");
        update();
    }

    function update() payable {
        emit LogUSDRate("Oraclize query was sent, waiting for
        the answer..");
        oraclize_query("URL","json(https://min-api.
        cryptocompare.com/data/price?fsym=ETH&tsyms=USD).USD");
    }

    function __callback(bytes32 _myid, string _result) {
        require (msg.sender == oraclize_cbAddress());
        emit LogUSDRate(_result);
        price = parseInt(_result, 2); // let's save it as $
        cents
    }

    function getPrice() constant returns (uint) {
        return price;
    }

}
```

Now compile and run to see the information in the event logs. But it does not work. It's worth noting that Oraclize is not compatible with the JavaScript VM on Remix. It can run with the mainnet, Rinkeby, Ropsten, and Kovan, but using a testnet for development is not recommended because that would require quite a bit of extra work. Thankfully, the Oraclize IDE can come to the rescue.

Trying the Oraclize IDE

Oraclize comes with its own browser-based IDE that is a patched version of Remix; you can find it at `http://dapps.oraclize.it/browser-solidity/`. You can also check out a few smart contracts that come as examples at `http://dapps.oraclize.it/browser-solidity/#gist=9817193e5b05206 847ed1fcd1d16bd1d`.

Go to `https://dev.oraclize.it/` and click the first link: "Web IDE & code samples." You will find four samples, listed in the order of complexity, as shown in Figure 6-2. Also, the readme section explains this well.

```
README.md    DieselPrice.sol ✕    KrakenPriceTicker.sol    WolframAlpha.sol    YoutubeViews.sol
/*
   Diesel Price Peg

   This contract keeps in storage a reference
   to the Diesel Price in USD
*/


pragma solidity ^0.4.0;
import "github.com/oraclize/ethereum-api/oraclizeAPI.sol";

contract DieselPrice is usingOraclize {

    uint public DieselPriceUSD;

    event newOraclizeQuery(string description);
    event newDieselPrice(string price);

    function DieselPrice() {
        update(); // first check at contract creation
    }

    function __callback(bytes32 myid, string result) {
        if (msg.sender != oraclize_cbAddress()) throw;
        newDieselPrice(result);
        DieselPriceUSD = parseInt(result, 2); // let's save it as $ cents
        // do something with the USD Diesel price
    }

    function update() payable {
        newOraclizeQuery("Oraclize query was sent, standing by for the answer..");
        oraclize_query("URL", "xml(https://www.fueleconomy.gov/ws/rest/fuelprices).fuelPrices.diesel");
    }

}
```

Figure 6-2. *Contracts on the* `https://dev.oraclize.it/` *web site*

On the right side, click the fourth tab icon, which represents Oraclize. You'll see a warning, as shown in Figure 6-3.

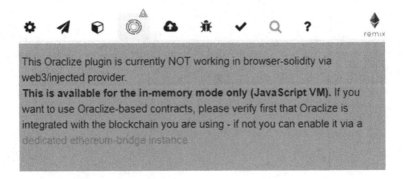

Figure 6-3. *Oraclize warning*

Now click the cube-shaped icon called Environment and choose JavaScript VM instead of Injected Web3. The warning will disappear.

Now create a new file and paste the same update code that was discussed earlier. You may come across some compilation issues on the right side, as shown in Figure 6-4.

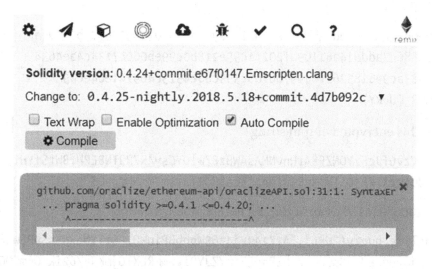

Figure 6-4. *Compilation issue on Oraclize*

This issue appeared previously to version 0.4.25-nightly.2018.8.16+ commit.a9e7ae29, but it's working perfectly as of that build. If this issue arises again, try changing the Solidity versions to previous ones to see if this works.

Encrypting Data with a Python Script

If the smart contract is on a public Ethereum blockchain network, then it's advisable to encrypt the query data for privacy. There are options so you can encrypt a single parameter or the entire query as per your needs.

Visit this web site to retrieve a CLI tool to encrypt the entire query: https://github.com/oraclize/encrypted-queries/blob/master/ tools/encrypted_queries_tools.py.

Using the CLI command, you can encrypt an arbitrary string of text, as shown here, by using the default Oraclize public key (the long string after the -p flag):

```
python encrypted_queries_tools.py -e -p 044992e9473b7d90ca
54d2886c7addd14a61109af202f1c95e218b0c99eb060c7134c4ae4634
5d0383ac996185762f04997d6fd6c393c86e4325c469741e64eca9
"YOUR QUERY"
```

This encrypted output string

```
BEIGVzv6fJcFiYQNZF8ArHnvNMAsAWBz8ZwlOYCsy4K/RJTN8ERHfBWtSfYHt+
uegdD1wtXTkP30sTW+3xR3w/un1i3caSOORfa+wmIMmNHt4aOS
```

can then be used as an argument for an Oraclize query.

```
oraclize_query("URL","AzK149Vj4z65WphbBPiuWQ2PStTINeVp5sS9PSwqZ
i8NsjQy6jJLH765qQu3U/ bZPNeEB/bYZJYBivwmmREXTGjmKJk/62ikcO6mIMQ
fB5jBVVUOqzzZ/A8ecWR2nOLvOCKkkkFzBYp2sW1H

31GI+SQzWV9q64WdqZsAa4gXqHb6jmLkVFjOGIOJvrA/
Zh6T5lyeLPSmaslI");
```

In this example, you have encrypted only one argument using the previous tool. This is called *partial encryption*. Now let's try to send an encrypted query to Oraclize whose original data is as shown in Listing 6-5. Here you use the previous tool to encrypt all the parameters individually and form the final query, keeping the values in the correct order.

Listing 6-5. Oraclize Query

```
oraclize_query("BEIGVzv6fJcFiYQNZF8ArHnvNMAsAWBz8ZwlOYCsy4K/
RJTN8ERHfBWtSfYHt+
    uegdD1wtXTkP3OsTW+3xR3w/un1i3caSOORfa+wmIMmNHt4aOS","BNKdFtmf
    mazLLR/bfey4mP8
    v/R5zCIUK7obcUrF2d6CWUMvKKUorQqYZNu1YfRZsGlp/
    F96CAQhSGomJC7oJa3PktwoW5J1Oti/y2v4+b5+vN8yLIj1trS7p1l341Jf66
    AjaxnoFPplwLqE=", "BF5u1td9ugoacDabyfVzoTxPBxG
    NtmXuGV7AFcO1GLmXkXIKlBcAcelvaTKIbmaA6lXwZCJCSeWDHJOirHiEl1
    LtR8lCt+1ISttWuvp
    J6sPx3Y/QxTajYzxZfQb6nCGkv+8cczXOPrqKKwOn/Elf9kpQQCXeMglunT
    O9H2B4HfRs7uuI");
```

Recursive Time-Based Queries

You can set a time-based query through Oraclize where you update the EUR/GBP exchange rate every 60 seconds, until the contract has enough funds to pay for the Oraclize fee (see Listing 6-6).

Listing 6-6. Time based oraclize query

```
oraclize_query(60, "URL", "json(http://api.fixer.io/
latest?symbols=USD,GBP).rates.GBP");
```

Oraclize Real-Life Implementations

Oraclize is widely used in the industry in Ethereum decentralized applications. At http://dapps.oraclize.it/, you can find a few examples of decentralized applications based on Oraclize and Ethereum.

ChainLink

ChainLink is the major competitor of Oraclize. The primary difference between the two is that Oraclize is centralized, whereas ChainLink is based on a decentralized platform and hence trustless and verifiable. You will find more examples of Oraclize because it's been on the market for longer and is more widely used by most of the blockchain frameworks. To learn more about ChainLink, you can visit https://chainlink-docs.smartcontract.com.

Storing Larger Content on IPFS

In previous chapters, we discussed that Ethereum in its current form is not the best place to store large amounts of data or PDF, Microsoft Word, and image files. For such content, you have to use an external IPFS server. Currently there's no built-in mechanism that would allow smart contracts to communicate with IPFS (or anything outside of Ethereum). To make those two things exchange data, first you will save the file in IPFS that will return a hash, and finally the hash will be saved to a Ethereum node against an address for reference and retrieval later.

Benefits of IPFS

You can use a regular RDBMS to store data and save only hashes of the transactions to Ethereum. However, using IPFS for saving data comes with its own benefits.

- *No duplication*: IPFS removes duplications across the network and tracks version history for every file. IPFS also provides high performance and clustered persistence.

- *Compatibility with Ethereum*: IPFS and the blockchain are a perfect match. You can address large amounts of data with IPFS and place the immutable, permanent

IPFS links into a blockchain transaction. This timestamps and secures your content, without having to put the data on the chain itself.

- *Cost*: IPFS brings the freedom and independent spirit of the Web at full force—and at low cost. IPFS can help deliver content in a way that can save you considerable money.

- *Bandwidth*: If your company delivers large amounts of data to users, a peer-to-peer approach could save you millions in bandwidth. IPFS can provide secure P2P content delivery.

Let's discuss the installation and programming of IPFS.

Locally Configuring IPFS

Install IPFS as per the instructions at `https://ipfs.io/docs/install/`.

1. Download the IPFS binaries from `https://dist.ipfs.io/#go-ipfs`.

2. Unzip the file and the structure of all the files, as shown in Figure 6-5.

3. You may need to update based on the current `install.exe` and `install.sh` files depending upon whether you're on Windows or macOS .

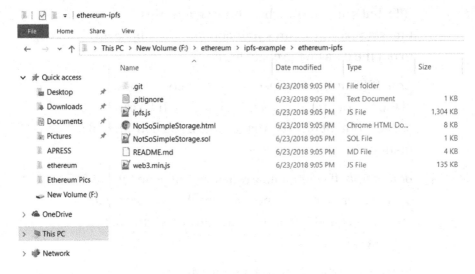

Figure 6-5. *File structure*

4. Set up the environment variable under the system
    path shown in Figure 6-6 so that `ipfs` commands
    can be run from anywhere.

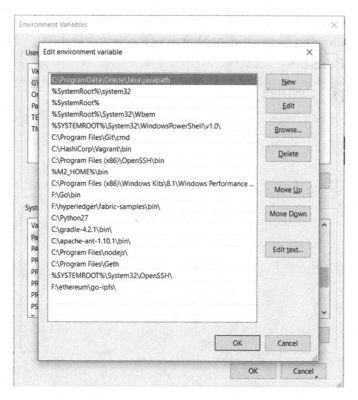

Figure 6-6. *Setting up the system path*

5. Run the following command. To check whether it's
    correctly deployed, the output console should look
    like Listing 6-7.

    ```
    ipfs version
    ```

Listing 6-7. IPFS version

```
F:\ethereum>ipfs version
ipfs version 0.4.15
```

6. You can find out all the commands on IPFS with the following command, as shown in Figure 6-7 and Listing 6-8.

```
ipfs commands
```

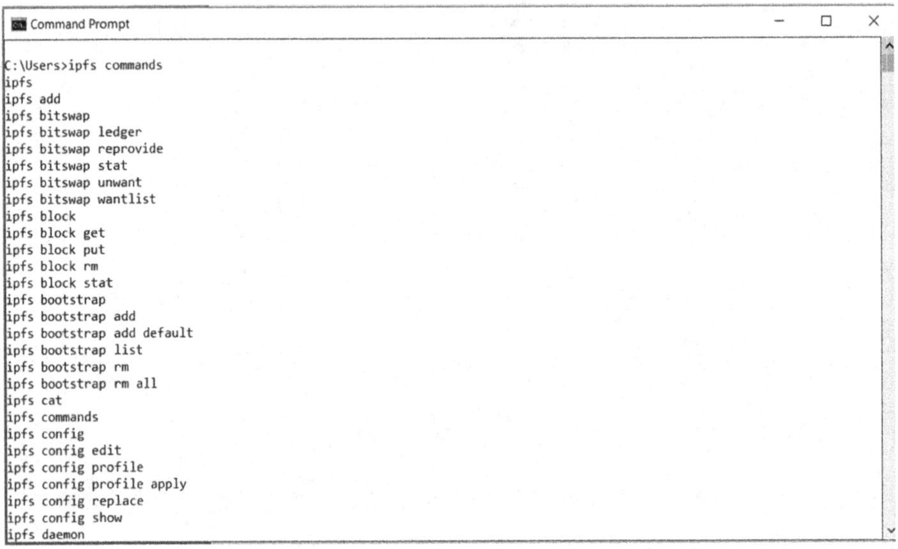

Figure 6-7. *ipfs commands*

Listing 6-8. IPFS commands

```
F:\ethereum>ipfs commands
ipfs
ipfs add
ipfs bitswap
ipfs bitswap ledger
ipfs bitswap reprovide
```

7. You can also see all the commands through the following command, as shown in Figure 6-8 and Listing 6-9:

```
ipfs help
```

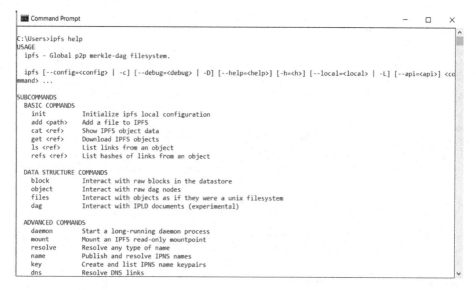

Figure 6-8. *ipfs help*

Listing 6-9. IPFS help output

```
F:\ethereum>ipfs help
USAGE
ipfs - Global p2p merkle-dag filesystem.

  ipfs [--config=<config> | -c] [--debug=<debug> | -D]
  [--help=<help>] [-h=<h>] [--local=<local> | -L] [--api=<api>]
  <command> ...
```

8. Initialize IPFS, as shown in Figure 6-9 and
    Listing 6-10. If you are on Windows, run all the next
    commands from the bash window.

    ```
    ipfs init
    ```

```
Devjani@DESKTOP-UHTA6E3 MINGW64 /f/ethereum/ipfs-example/ethereum-ipfs (master)
$ export IPFS_PATH=.ipfs

Devjani@DESKTOP-UHTA6E3 MINGW64 /f/ethereum/ipfs-example/ethereum-ipfs (master)
$ echo $IPFS_PATH
.ipfs

Devjani@DESKTOP-UHTA6E3 MINGW64 /f/ethereum/ipfs-example/ethereum-ipfs (master)
$ ipfs init
initializing IPFS node at .ipfs
generating 2048-bit RSA keypair...done
peer identity: QmPGx16WcXGWp2bTgusV5xsDgRn83XoHfbN1M7Zq3eCBYv
to get started, enter:

        ipfs cat /ipfs/QmS4ustL54uo8FzR9455qaxZwuMiUhyvMcX9Ba8nUH4uVv/readme


Devjani@DESKTOP-UHTA6E3 MINGW64 /f/ethereum/ipfs-example/ethereum-ipfs (master)
$ ipfs config --json API.HTTPHeaders.Access-Control-Allow-Origin '["*"]'

Devjani@DESKTOP-UHTA6E3 MINGW64 /f/ethereum/ipfs-example/ethereum-ipfs (master)
$ ipfs config --json Gateway.HTTPHeaders.Access-Control-Allow-Origin '["*"]'
```

Figure 6-9. ipfs commands

Listing 6-10. IPFS cat command

```
$ ipfs init
initializing IPFS node at .ipfs
generating 2048-bit RSA keypair...done
peer identity: QmPGx16WcXGWp2bTgusV5xsDgRn83XoHfbN1M7Zq3eCBYv
to get started, enter:

        ipfs cat /ipfs/
        QmS4ustL54uo8FzR9455qaxZwuMiUhyvMcX9Ba8nUH4uVv/readme
```

Note   This command has to be run only once. If you run it again, it will throw warnings.

---

9. Now you have to enable cross-origin resource sharing (CORS) on the IPFS node with the following commands. CORS is enabled so that all requests will be allowed.

```
ipfs config --jsonAPI.HTTPHeaders.Access-Control-Allow-
Origin '["*"]'
ipfs config --jsonGateway.HTTPHeaders.Access-Control-
Allow-Origin '["*"]'
```

Note Cross-origin resource sharing is a mechanism that allows restricted resources (e.g., fonts) on a web page to be requested from another domain outside the domain from which the first resource was served. A web page may freely embed cross-origin images, style sheets, scripts, iframes, and videos.

---

10. Now you can run the following command to run the server (if you're on Windows, run this in bash mode):

     ```
     ipfs daemon
     ```

     The output will look like Listing 6-11.

Listing 6-11. IPFS daemon command output

```
$ ipfs daemon
Initializing daemon...
Swarm listening on /ip4/10.0.75.1/tcp/4001
Swarm listening on /ip4/127.0.0.1/tcp/4001
Swarm listening on /ip4/169.254.164.245/tcp/4001
Swarm listening on /ip4/169.254.170.245/tcp/4001
Swarm listening on /ip4/169.254.189.121/tcp/4001
Swarm listening on /ip4/169.254.230.188/tcp/4001
Swarm listening on /ip4/172.18.160.1/tcp/4001
Swarm listening on /ip4/192.168.1.6/tcp/4001
Swarm listening on /ip4/192.168.51.129/tcp/4001
```

```
Swarm listening on /ip6/::1/tcp/4001
Swarm listening on /p2p-circuit/ipfs/
QmPGx16WcXGWp2bTgusV5xsDgRn83XoHfbN1M7Zq3eCBYv
Swarm announcing /ip4/10.0.75.1/tcp/4001
Swarm announcing /ip4/127.0.0.1/tcp/4001
Swarm announcing /ip4/169.254.164.245/tcp/4001
Swarm announcing /ip4/169.254.170.245/tcp/4001
Swarm announcing /ip4/169.254.189.121/tcp/4001
Swarm announcing /ip4/169.254.230.188/tcp/4001
Swarm announcing /ip4/172.18.160.1/tcp/4001
Swarm announcing /ip4/192.168.1.6/tcp/4001
Swarm announcing /ip4/192.168.51.129/tcp/4001
Swarm announcing /ip6/::1/tcp/4001
API server listening on /ip4/127.0.0.1/tcp/5001
Gateway (readonly) server listening on /ip4/127.0.0.1/tcp/8080
Daemon is ready
```

11. Now run the following command to find all the
     peers that will share the contents you are uploading
     to IPFS storage:

     ```
     ipfs swarm peers
     ```

     The output will look like Listing 6-12.

Listing 6-12. IPFS swarm peers list on console output

```
$ ipfs swarm peers
/ip4/100.34.210.63/tcp/14655/ipfs/
QmPRa5sovWPGhSDuEGU2cgfws5ra91bD89xTWmArJxickp
/ip4/100.38.242.117/tcp/24885/ipfs/
QmfGpAZPq1br1G6Q9KcLNqGKLnRjjmXvc6BD5yFfRVQv2y
```

12. Now create a folder and add an image called E.jpeg
     to it. Go to that folder and execute the following
     command:

     ```
     ipfs add -r .
     ```

     The output will look like Listing 6-13.

Listing 6-13. IPFS command to add files console output

```
$ ipfs add -r .
added QmbFDRLYyZaaTv3EJmz2QGtUFpvDT9rM7xPQrQkjUuX4qc images/E.
jpeg
added QmUFVahZy2eLbyVqjxK47aoSCDW1MGzoCig5VA4z3sTMAD images
```

     Now publish this file through the following
     command with the hash value shown earlier:

     ```
     ipfs name publish
     QmUFVahZy2eLbyVqjxK47aoSCDW1MGzoCig5VA4z3sTMAD
     ```

     The output will look like Listing 6-14.

Listing 6-14. IPFS command to publish file console output

```
$ ipfs name publish
QmUFVahZy2eLbyVqjxK47aoSCDW1MGzoCig5VA4z3sTMAD
Published to QmPGx16WcXGWp2bTgusV5xsDgRn83XoHfbN1M7Zq3eCBYv: /
ipfs/QmUFVahZy2eLbyVqjxK47aoSCDW1MGzoCig5VA4z3sTMAD
```

     Now you can surf this image on the IPFS web site
     using this URL: https://gateway.ipfs.io/ipfs/
     QmUFVahZy2eLbyVqjxK47aoSCDW1MGzoCig5VA4z3s
     TMAD. As shown in Figure 6-10, this contains the
     hash value returned by IPFS. This URL can be stored
     on Ethereum nodes as a string and accessed per
     your needs.

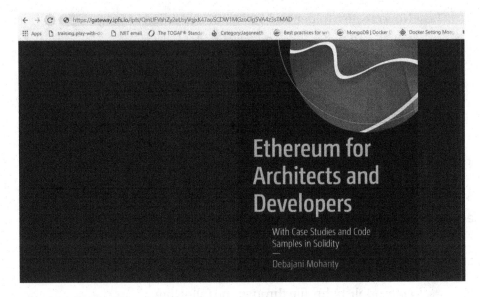

Figure 6-10. *File added to IPFS storage*

IPNS

IPNS is the equivalent of DNS for IPFS. The files on IPFS can always be
retrieved through a hash; however, if you forget the hash, you can access
it through the name provided by IPNS. Also, if you make some changes
to your file already saved to IPFS, then any retrieval from IPFS will point
to the original version of the file. IPFS uses hashes that point to a specific
version of the file like a committed hash in Git. That's why IPNS is
needed. Adding a file to IPNS will return a peer ID, and in the future any
reference to the peer ID will always return the latest version. The peer
ID will not change with different versions of the file. You can visit this
web site to learn more about how to use IPNS for storing files on IPFS:
`https://medium.com/coinmonks/how-to-add-site-to-ipfs-and-ipns-`
`f121b4cfc8ee`.

Ethereum Best Practices

Many business leaders have reported that even when they developed a best-of-class blockchain solution in a particular business vertical following all the best practices mentioned in this chapter, still they found no buyers. They note that no client would agree to transform their existing core bread-and-butter systems to a blockchain Dapp overnight. Rather, I advise you to start with a small, noncrucial area of your business or even conceptualize a new use case. Specifically, here are some best-practice steps:

1. Study the working model of your existing clients.

2. Brainstorm and find out use cases that are small, are sellable, and yet would add value to customer.

3. Choose the ecosystem carefully after considering the cost of the cryptocurrency such as fuel, licenses, development, cloud options, and so on.

4. Develop and write enough unit testing to cover all scenarios.

5. Run on the test framework. Do functional testing.

6. Involve the client throughout your blockchain journey and demonstration.

7. Implement in production.

8. If possible, consider the cloud to cut down on the costs.

The previous suggestions are pretty generic and are applicable to almost any system. Let's go step-by-step to discuss best practices that you should follow in the blockchain journey.

Enterprise Smart Contracts

Most smart contracts are deployed in a public network and they communicate with the external world where anyone can attack your contract and manipulate it if the transactions in the code are not handled with caution. Also, working yet insufficient code may end up losing a lot of your money from your wallet. At the same time, any bug in the existing code could prove fatal for your business as well as for the client contracts invoking your code if not paid proper, early attention. Some of the vulnerabilities are discussed in the following sections.

Version

The first line in the Solidity file (`pragma solidity ^0.4.0;`) signifies the compiler version. If you write `^0.4.0`, it refers to the latest version of version 0.4.*x* series. However, it's advisable to set the version to `pragma solidity 0.4.4;` to minimize any compilation issues that may incur if you keep the minor versions open. Also, many of the previous issues have been sorted out in version 0.4, and hence it's a good idea to use this version or later. Also, before adopting a particular version, it's a good idea to read about all the new updates as well as the limitations and known bugs of that release and handle them in your code accordingly.

Naming Conventions

The events and functions should be named properly so that they clearly indicate their purpose.

It's a good practice to have an event's name start with `Event` or `Log`, as in `event EventMoneyTransfer()`, `event LogMoneyTransfer()`, and so on.

Similarly, while calling external services, name the contract and functions accordingly because they are the riskiest part of the code and should be marked through naming conventions accordingly. The name should start with `UnTrusted` or `External` and so on.

Visibility Call

Use the proper visibility for functions and variables in your code, either external, public, private, or internal. Unless required, use the minimum visibilities to safeguard your code from external attacks.

Delegate Call

With a delegate call, a contract can invoke another contract at runtime and change the values of the public variables of the contract invoked. This is another reason why you must use public and external visibility only when required. Also, all variables at the contract level should have private or internal visibility.

Simplicity and Modularity

It's always advisable to keep your contract simple and modular. It's good to keep the code modular; in other words, different functionalities should be kept in a separate contract file so that it can be updated independently without impacting the whole code. Also, modularity will minimize duplication and improve reusability. Especially the data part should be kept in a separate file because it can change more frequently than the business logic in some business verticals. Also, use libraries and tools for functionalities that are already available rather than coding them yourself.

Overflow and Underflow

This is a common pitfall that can lead to big issues if not handled properly. You know that all integer and byte values have minimum and maximum values. If you do not have a check in the code, then the value may surpass the boundaries. OpenZeppelin's SafeMath library (`https://github.com/ OpenZeppelin/openzeppelin-solidity/blob/master/contracts/math/ SafeMath.sol`) can help you here to handle this issue.

External Calls

You need to be extra careful during external calls because they can involve encountering security risks, losing gas, and throwing errors. Choose carefully between the send(), transfer(), and call.value() functions and understand their pros and cons in detail. The functions send() and transfer() prevent reentrancy; however, they are incompatible with any contract whose fallback function requires more than 2,300 gas.

Race Conditions

External calls are always risky because they can control your own smart contract by manipulating data that the function was not expecting. Some of the related issues are reentrancy, timestamp dependency, and transaction ordering. Let's discuss them one by one.

Reentrancy

A computer program or function is reentrant if it can be invoked by multiple users at the same time sharing a common memory. In an Ethereum network, all transactions should be atomic in nature. In the case of errors or exceptions, the whole thing should be rolled back safely, and the gas should be restored to owner. However, reentrancy still is a danger because when you call an external contract on which you have no control, that contract may call your contract and manipulate the data before your function has finished running. This may lead to infinite looping at times.

Also, even in your own contract, the functions and variables should be of minimum visibility and should be initialized at the beginning of functions to minimize race conditions. Consider the code in Listing 6-15.

Listing 6-15. Risky code

```
// Bad
mapping (address => uint) private userAmount;
function withdrawAmount() public {
uint amountToWithdraw = userAmount[msg.sender];
if (!(msg.sender.call.value(amountToWithdraw)())) { throw; }
        // At this point, the function withdrawAmount() is
        called again
        userAmount[msg.sender] = 0;
}
```

If the if function in Listing 6-15 is called multiple times in quick succession, then the second call may withdraw the balance over and over again before the first call finishes.

As shown in Listing 6-16, it's a good idea to update the value early in the program. Also, use send() instead of call.value() to prevent any external code from being executed.

Listing 6-16. Good practice to update value early in program

```
// Good
mapping (address => uint) private userAmount;
function withdrawAmount() public {
        uint amountToWithdraw = userAmount[msg.sender];
        userAmount[msg.sender] = 0;
        if (!(msg.sender.call.value(amountToWithdraw)())) {
        throw; }
        // At this point, the caller's code is executed, and
        can call withdrawAmount() again
}
```

But do not worry because standard IDEs such as Remix will give you a warning for reentrancy, and you have to fix it during development.

Timestamp Dependence

In a public Ethereum blockchain network, the timestamp can be manipulated by the miner and hence should not be used for critical components of the contract. Especially for timestamp-based seed generators for gaming software, the code can be manipulated to great extent by miner. Be careful in this area.

Transaction Ordering

A transaction ordering attack is a type of race condition attack where the miner manipulates the price of the transaction by reordering the transactions and the order of mining. As a result, the actual price gets updated at runtime while processing it. So, the transaction owner ends up paying a different amount than expected.

Token Standards

There is no standard or best practice that is final for Solidity as the entire ecosystem has yet to mature. However, it's a good idea to adhere to the EIP tokens such as ECR20 that are followed by developers in this field. It gives a common language of communication between contracts across different parties.

Unit Testing

Writing unit tests may seem like a lot of work; however, it will save you from bigger issues that could be discovered much later. A serious bug in production could prove much more expensive for business than to find them early in the code and fix them well ahead of going live. Hence, all possible positive, negative, and boundary conditions should be covered by using unit testing. Also, use a standard Solidity code coverage tool such as SolCover or Solidity-coverage (`https://github.com/sc-forks/solidity-coverage`) and always strive for a higher percentage of coverage of each piece of code every time you add or update.

Smart Contract Auditing

A good amount of auditing and peer reviews can save a lot of issues that may incur over time. Establish a good coding standard for your development team, and review the overall architecture of the contract and safe usage of third-party smart contracts early in the project to ensure the contract is structured in a way that will not result in current or future issues. Use automated tools, purposefully designed to test the security of the contract. Data flow and control flow should also be analyzed to identify vulnerabilities.

Security Tools

We already discussed SolCover for unit testing coverage. In addition, you can use the Oyente analysis tool for finding vulnerabilities in a smart contract. Also, the Solgraph tool can generate a DOT graph for you to indicate the flow of the Solidity smart contract and potential security vulnerabilities in it.

CHAPTER 7

Frameworks: Truffle and Embark

"As society becomes more and more complex, cheating will in many ways become progressively easier and easier to do and harder to police or even understand."

—Vitalik Buterin

So far we have discussed the Ethereum architecture, Solidity programming, and the Ethereum client, including setting it up and compiling, running, and debugging Dapps. That's a lot of work, isn't it? In this chapter, let's discuss two leading frameworks, Truffle and Embark, that will provide a set of tools and boilerplate code for scaffolding Dapps for Ethereum. The frameworks will do much of the work themselves and leave you with only a few tasks.

Truffle

Truffle claims to be a "world-class development environment, testing framework, and asset pipeline for Ethereum, aiming to make life as an Ethereum developer easier."

© Debajani Mohanty 2018
D. Mohanty, *Ethereum for Architects and Developers*,
https://doi.org/10.1007/978-1-4842-4075-5_7

Install Truffle

Truffle is a node package and can be set up in seconds by running the node command on Windows, Linux, or macOS.

```
npm install -g truffle
```

By adding -g, you are installing Truffle globally. To test a contract created using Truffle, you will need to do it locally by running the ganache-cli command or through an Ethereum client. For now let's use ganache-cli.

Create a Truffle Project

Creating a Truffle project is painless and super quick. Create a folder called myTruffle, go to the folder, and run the command shown here:

```
truffle init
```

Figure 7-1 shows the result.

```
F:\ethereum\myTruffle>truffle init
Downloading project...
Project initialized.

  Documentation: http://truffleframework.com/docs

Commands:

  Compile: truffle compile
  Migrate: truffle migrate
  Test:    truffle test


F:\ethereum\myTruffle>
```

Figure 7-1. *Running truffle init*

In a few seconds, this will create a template project for you, as shown in Figure 7-2.

- The `contracts` folder is where the smart contracts written in Solidity are stored.

- The `migrations` folder contains scripts to manage the deployment of contracts onto the Ethereum network.

- The `test` folder is where you write all your unit tests to test your smart contracts.

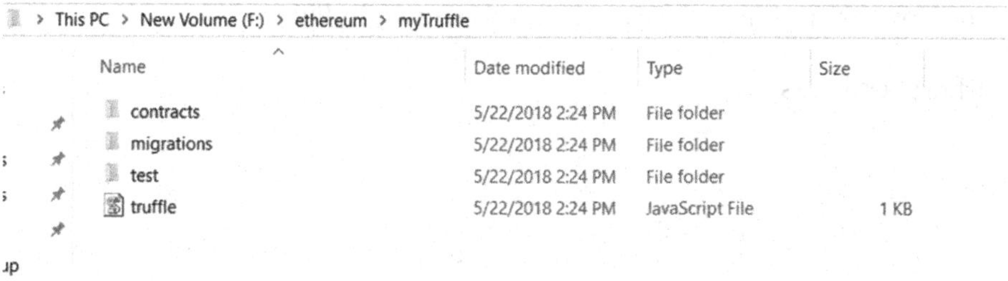

> This PC > New Volume (F:) > ethereum > myTruffle				
Name	^	Date modified	Type	Size
contracts		5/22/2018 2:24 PM	File folder	
migrations		5/22/2018 2:24 PM	File folder	
test		5/22/2018 2:24 PM	File folder	
truffle		5/22/2018 2:24 PM	JavaScript File	1 KB

Figure 7-2. *Truffle project structure*

`truffle-config.js` is also created as part of the `truffle init` command. Now you can compile the default project and then test it through the following commands. You can gradually update this default project and smart contract as per your needs.

```
truffle compile
truffle test
truffle deploy
```

Note that in Windows you may encounter an issue. Hence, add a `.cmd` extension to the `truffle` command, as shown here:

```
truffle.cmd compile
```

183

Figure 7-3 shows the result of the `truffle.cmd compile` command.

```
F:\ethereum\myTruffle>truffle.cmd compile
Compiling .\contracts\ConvertLib.sol...
Compiling .\contracts\MetaCoin.sol...
Compiling .\contracts\Migrations.sol...
Writing artifacts to .\build\contracts
```

Figure 7-3. *truffle compile*

The following command will unit test the `MyContract.sol` contract for some positive and negative scenarios, as shown in Figure 7-4:

```
truffle.cmd test
```

```
TestMetacoin
  √ testInitialBalanceUsingDeployedContract (107ms)
  √ testInitialBalanceWithNewMetaCoin (83ms)

Contract: MetaCoin
  √ should put 10000 MetaCoin in the first account
  √ should call a function that depends on a linked library (124ms)
  √ should send coin correctly (156ms)


5 passing (1s)


F:\ethereum\myTruffle>_
```

Figure 7-4. *truffle test*

The following command will deploy the `MyContract.sol` contract, as shown in Figure 7-5:

```
truffle.cmd deploy
```

```
F:\ethereum\myTruffle>truffle.cmd deploy
Using network 'development'.

Running migration: 1_initial_migration.js
  Deploying Migrations...
  ... 0x1fc6008075209fea546c2310e8384bce13d52ea5802812ed25e295a5147ed351
  Migrations: 0x0c8eb5ea73d701f0b55fb8342f6c0c749ad00140
Saving successful migration to network...
  ... 0xf60296fb1f8c4fd93124ab666aa5a0735a1e9b0cf99791a96c5035625adc81d8
Saving artifacts...
Running migration: 2_deploy_contracts.js
  Deploying ConvertLib...
  ... 0x9a48f71b5baaef6417762ee2a755c5bb58db0708d06527ec0a4e1e978561625d
  ConvertLib: 0xcf97b5cd1c6a402beee653b6dbbb2a4ba9a974ad
  Linking ConvertLib to MetaCoin
  Deploying MetaCoin...
  ... 0xee875b374a99cc7137ebea40c587802ce38e37dcab0829e90407721e2529dd65
  MetaCoin: 0xed2536a3e192996fbf0991deec8aea59ac1b378b
Saving successful migration to network...
  ... 0x0414aaf4442206a5f3a717756b0be8ae2eee24792d0177308c091642acb84397
Saving artifacts...
```

Figure 7-5. *truffle deploy*

Provided MetaMask is already installed on your Chrome browser and ganache-cli is already running in the background, you can check the Truffle Dapp in your browser by visiting http://localhost:8080.

Now that you know how simple it is, why don't you start coding with Truffle on your own?

If you're still not sure, try the Pet Shop example on the Truffle web site, available at https://truffleframework.com/tutorials/pet-shop.

Unit Testing

If you want to write good unit testing, you can check out these two web sites:

https://truffleframework.com/tutorials/solidity-unit-tests
https://truffleframework.com/docs/getting_started/testing

Now let's try something on your own. Listing 7-1 shows a smart contract named MyContract.Sol.

Listing 7-1. MyContract.Sol

```solidity
pragma solidity ^0.4.0;

contract MyContract {
    uint private amount;

    function MyContract()
    {
        amount = 101;
    }

    function updateAmount(uint newAmount)
        public
        returns (bool success)
    {
      require(newAmount > 100); /* Contract stores numbers
      greater than 100. */
      amount = newAmount;
      return true;
    }

    function getAmount()
        public
        returns (uint)
    {
        return amount;
      }
}
```

Save the MyContract.Sol code to the contracts folder of the myTruffle project you created earlier.

Now within the test folder, paste `MyContractTest.Sol` as shown in Listing 7-2. This unit testing code checks the `MyContract.Sol` file for an initial value, which is 101, and for two other values, 97 and 122. For value 97, the contract should throw an exception because the `require` condition is used.

Listing 7-2. MyContractTest.Sol

```solidity
pragma solidity ^0.4.0;

import "truffle/Assert.sol";
import "truffle/DeployedAddresses.sol";
import "../contracts/MyContract.sol";

contract MyContractTest {

function testInitialStoredValue() {
        MyContract mycontract = new MyContract();
        uint expected = 101;
        Assert.equal(mycontract.getAmount(), expected,
        "Initial amount set should be 101.");
   }

function testTheThrow() {
        MyContract mycontract = new MyContract();
        ThrowProxy throwproxy = new ThrowProxy(address(myco
        ntract));
        MyContract(address(throwproxy)).updateAmount(97);
        bool r = throwproxy.execute.gas(200000)();
        Assert.isFalse(r, "Should be false because is
        should throw!");
   }
```

```solidity
function testNoThrow() {
        MyContract mycontract = new MyContract();
        ThrowProxy throwproxy = new ThrowProxy(address(myco
        ntract));
        MyContract(address(throwproxy)).updateAmount(122);
        bool r = throwproxy.execute.gas(200000)();
        Assert.isTrue(r, "Should be true!");
    }
}

// Proxy contract for testing throws
contract ThrowProxy {
  address public target;
  bytes data;

  function ThrowProxy(address _target) {
    target = _target;
  }

  //prime the data using the fallback function.
  function() {
    data = msg.data;
  }

  function execute() returns (bool) {
    return target.call(data);
  }
}
```

Make sure ganache-cli is running in the background. Now run the following commands again:

```
truffle compile
```

For Windows, use `truffle.cmd compile` instead. If everything goes well, it won't show any output.

```
truffle test
```
Similarly use "truffle.cmd test" for windows.

You can see whether the tests pass or fail on the command line, as shown in Figure 7-6 and Listing 7-3.

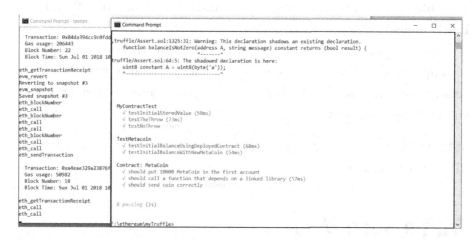

Figure 7-6. *Truffle unit testing*

Listing 7-3. Truffle unit testing

```
F:\ethereum\myTruffle>truffle.cmd test
Using network 'development'.

Compiling .\contracts\ConvertLib.sol...
Compiling .\contracts\MetaCoin.sol...
Compiling .\contracts\MyContract.sol...
Compiling .\test\MyContractTest.sol...
Compiling .\test\TestMetacoin.sol...
Compiling .\test\TestMyContract.sol...
Compiling truffle/Assert.sol...
Compiling truffle/DeployedAddresses.sol...
```

OpenZeppelin: Securing Solidity Code

Smart contracts deployed in public networks are susceptible to loads of risk because money is involved. Zeppelin, which started as a smart contract auditing service, has added a layer of security for your Solidity smart contracts deployed on public Ethereum blockchains. Its product OpenZeppelin claims to be a "battle-tested framework of reusable smart contracts for Ethereum and other EVM and eWASM blockchains."

OpenZeppelin integrates with Truffle. Especially when your code is complex and involves loops and the possibility of failures while calling an external service, OpenZepplin is a good option to overcome vulnerabilities. You can try it yourself; learn more here:

```
https://truffleframework.com/tutorials/robust-smart-contracts-
with-openzeppelin
```

Truffle Road Map

Here is an interesting road map of Truffle in the near future:

- Truffle 4.0 will come with a debugger, an improved development and testing experience, and more.

- Drizzle is a front-end framework for React and Angular that will easily connect to Truffle-based projects.

- Project Hotcakes is a full-stack suite for web applications.

- Live is a browser-based, interactive Truffle IDE.

Embark

Though Truffle claims to be the "most popular development framework for Ethereum with a mission to make your life a whole lot easier," I found Embark equally good. In fact, many features that I was looking for elsewhere on the Internet appear in Embark. The integration with IPFS is well explained, and the unit testing is just superb. Now it's time to try it.

Install Embark

Let's install and run the sample project from the Embark web site. Follow these steps:

1. Install Embark.

    ```
    npm -g install embark
    ```

2. If you already have the previous version embark-framework, then uninstall it and install the new one.

    ```
    npm uninstall -g embark-framework
    then
    npm install -g embark
    ```

Create an Embark Project

Now run the following on the command line, as shown in Figure 7-7 and Listing 7-4, and it will create a project template called embark_demo for you:

```
embark demo
```

```
F:\ethereum\embark>embark demo
Initializing Embark Template....
Installing packages...
Init complete

App ready at embark_demo
--------------------
Next steps:
-> cd embark_demo
-> embark blockchain or embark simulator
open another console in the same directory and run
-> embark run
For more info go to http://embark.status.im

F:\ethereum\embark>_
```

Figure 7-7. *Creating embark_demo*

Listing 7-4. Creating embark_demo

```
F:\ethereum\embark>embark demo
Initializing Embark Template....
Installing packages...
Init complete

App ready at embark_demo
--------------------
Next steps:
-> cd embark_demo
-> embark blockchain or embark simulator
   open another console in the same directory and run
-> embark run
For more info go to http://embark.status.im
```

Go to that folder and run the following command to run ganache-cli, as shown in Figure 7-8 and Listing 7-5:

```
embark simulator
```

```
▨ Command Prompt - embark simulator

F:\ethereum\embark\embark_demo>embark simulator
Ganache CLI v6.1.8 (ganache-core: 2.2.1)

Available Accounts
==================
(0) 0xb8d851486d1c953e31a44374aca11151d49b8bb3 (~100 ETH)
(1) 0xf6d5c6d500cac10ee7e6efb5c1b479cfb789950a (~100 ETH)
(2) 0xf09324e7a1e2821c2f7a4a47675f9cf0b1a5eb7f (~100 ETH)
(3) 0xfbaf82a227dcebd2f9334496658801f63299ba24 (~100 ETH)
(4) 0x774b5341944deac70199a4750556223cb008949b (~100 ETH)
(5) 0x4801428dad07e7c2401d033d195116011fc4e400 (~100 ETH)
(6) 0xcf08befbc01a5b02ea09d840797d6b4565d4d535 (~100 ETH)
(7) 0x1a2f3b98e434c02363f3dac3174af93c1d690914 (~100 ETH)
(8) 0x4a17f35f0a9927fb4141aa91cbbc72c1b31598de (~100 ETH)
(9) 0xdf18cb4f2005bc52f94e9bd6c31f7b0c6394e2c2 (~100 ETH)

Private Keys
==================
(0) 0xf942d5d524ec07158df4354402bfba8d928c99d0ab34d0799a6158d56156d986
(1) 0x88f37cfbaed8c0c515c62a17a3a1ce2f397d08bbf20dcc788b69f11b5a5c9791
(2) 0xf4ebc8adae40bfc741b0982c206061878bffed3ad1f34d67c94fa32c3d33eac8
(3) 0xca67021a16478270ede4fddd65d0c031c75cd36c13b6a56bcb767928c1c2cf86
(4) 0x9955b1e01b2a7d8c22df41754d48b08dff3c0f3dd79d43e091c6311f97f0605a
(5) 0x130137aa9a7fbc7cadc98c079cda47a999ff41931d9feaab621855beceed71f7
(6) 0xead83d04f741d2b3ab50be1299c18aa1a82c241606861a9a6d3122443496522d
(7) 0xe6e893ac9f1c1db066a8a83a376554084b0a786e4cdcd91559d68bd4a1dac396
(8) 0xf1023ac6c8695f6ceb5331a382be8846bfe078b22c18ad7ef4fc3ea6e1cc59e4
(9) 0x4aef59c2cf29479b2c27a5f208e6b89d65d16f4977988151e135460db8274fdb
```

Figure 7-8. *Embark simulator*

Listing 7-5. Embark Simulator

```
F:\ethereum\embark\embark_demo>embark simulator
Ganache CLI v6.1.8 (ganache-core: 2.2.1)

Available Accounts
==================
(0) 0xb8d851486d1c953e31a44374aca11151d49b8bb3 (~100 ETH)
(1) 0xf6d5c6d500cac10ee7e6efb5c1b479cfb789950a (~100 ETH)
```

(2) 0xf09324e7a1e2821c2f7a4a47675f9cf0b1a5eb7f (~100 ETH)

(3) 0xfbaf82a227dcebd2f9334496658801f63299ba24 (~100 ETH)

You can also run the following to run a real node:

`embark blockChain`

From another window from the same folder, run the following, and you will see the console, as shown in Figure 7-9 and Listing 7-6:

`embark run`

Figure 7-9. *Running embark run*

Listing 7-6. Running embark run

```
deploying contracts
 | deploying SimpleStorage with 134157 gas
 | SimpleStorage deployed at
   0x04D45b51fe4f00b4478F8b0719Fa779f14c8A194
 | finished deploying contracts
 | ready to watch file changes
 | webserver available at http://localhost:8000
```

The server is now running over port 8000 on local. Let's open `http://localhost:8000` in the browser and check the web console, as shown in Figure 7-10.

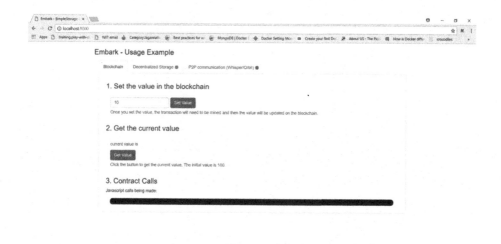

Figure 7-10. Embark running on local

Unit Testing

Note that the contracts are located in the `contracts` folder and the unit tests are in the `test` folder. The default project already comes with a contract called `simple_storage.sol` in the `contracts` folder.

Also note that the unit tests are written in JavaScript here, which is great news for JavaScript developers. Open the `simple_storage_spec.js` file in the `test` folder that comes by default and add more contracts as well as tests to learn more.

CHAPTER 8

Testing Strategy for Ethereum Dapps

"Blockchain software companies may end up being amalgamated into existing software giants, at which point blockchain patents will just become part of the existing patent war."

—Vitalik Buterin

Nowadays cutting-edge technologies such as machine learning, analytics, artificial intelligence, the cloud, and the blockchain are entering the marketplace at an unprecedented speed. The blockchain is one of the forerunners among them and is considered to be the next tech disruptor. According to a survey by the World Economic Forum, 10 percent of the global GDP will be relying on blockchain-based technology by 2027.

So far we have discussed the architecture, frameworks, development, unit testing, and deployment of Ethereum Dapps. I wonder why not many documents are available on the Internet about the testing strategy for this emerging technology. In fact, testing an Ethereum Dapp is not much different from any other application you would test. The same logic and critical thinking you already use for testing nonblockchain projects still apply. However, you should have a testing strategy that considers the functional and nonfunctional aspects of the testing.

© Debajani Mohanty 2018
D. Mohanty, *Ethereum for Architects and Developers*,
https://doi.org/10.1007/978-1-4842-4075-5_8

Blockchains and Testing

The testing of blockchain Dapps can be divided into two categories.

- Testing blockchains in a public network

- Testing blockchains in a private network

In both cases, the blockchain limits the role of the middleman because parties can safely share and update data in a distributed ledger.

Functional and Nonfunctional Testing

In a public blockchain, the miners are already doing half of the testing job for you. In other words, they check and validate data in the entire blockchain every time a new block is added. In a private blockchain, the chances of forgery are minor. So, the functional testing of blockchain-based Dapps in a way is different from testing an application running on a centralized database.

However, when it comes to nonfunctional testing, blockchain applications will demand the standard testing and validations, including performance tests, integration tests, security tests, and so on. In addition, there are a few special kinds of testing that are to be used solely for blockchain Dapps. Let's explore them.

Standard Functional Testing

Just like any other application, a blockchain-based decentralized application can be tested for all its functionalities; this includes unit testing, integration testing, and UI testing. This part is rather straightforward.

Unit Tests

Before a Dapp even reaches the testers, it is advisable that the developers follow best practices while coding and write enough unit tests to cover all scenarios in a smart contract. This is something I have already covered in previous chapters.

Unit tests are a type of white-box testing; they save a lot of time by analyzing functionality at the lowest levels and in the smallest chunks of functionality. The majority of bugs can be found early during the development phase and will not reach the user acceptance testing phase or production, avoiding potential bigger investments to fix the issue.

Integration Testing

A blockchain may consist of many different smart contracts deployed in public and private networks and even may communicate with databases as well as external systems such as IPFS or Oraclize. Hence, integration testing is essential to check the end-to-end working of the entire system in positive and negative scenarios.

User Interface and Mobile Apps Testing

User interface (UI) testing for Dapps is similar to any other UI testing that is done for traditional web applications on desktops and mobile devices with different browsers. Besides the cosmetic changes, the UI should be tested for performance and scalability and whether it's able to cope well with Dapps running in the background.

Standard Nonfunctional Testing

Nonfunctional testing in a blockchain is a hot topic for discussion as the industry is still not mature in this area and different blockchain platform companies are working on tools and benchmarks.

Security Testing

Because the blockchain boasts of being a secure immutable ledger, security testing is of special importance to blockchain Dapps. Using the right kind of hashing and identifying whether there is any piece in the entire application that is vulnerable to malicious attacks are the major responsibilities of testers; this is in addition to regular authentication, authorization, role-based testing, data confidentiality, and data integrity.

Load, Performance, and Stress Testing

We all know that public blockchain Dapps such as Bitcoin and Ethereum are extremely slow in comparison to their decentralized siblings. That puts additional burden on the tester to perform enough load testing, performance testing, and stress testing to identify any vulnerabilities, performance bottlenecks, network latencies, and so on. Setting up metrics for the Dapps as an indicator is desirable to evaluate to what extent the system can be loaded and still serve without any slowdown before complete disaster. Such data will help developers further fine-tune the coding, configuration, and so on. This will also set an expectation for the business for its contractual agreements before the Dapp goes to production.

Specialized Testing

So far the tests discussed are more or less similar in most software applications. Now let's discuss some of the tests specific to the Ethereum ecosystem.

Smart Contract Testing

At the core of the Ethereum ecosystem, run the smart contracts that deal with both the business logic and the data associated with it. Testing smart contracts in all positive and negative scenarios is desirable for the tester. Visit this web site to learn more: `https://ethereum.gitbooks.io/frontier-guide/content/testing_contracts_and_transactions.html`.

Node Testing

Testing the block size, chain size, data transfer, and encryption of data is vital for blockchain-based Dapps. It is also a good practice to automate the testing of the entire ecosystem.

Network Simulation Testing

Study the network behavior by simulating the way smart contracts will operate once in production and figure out the answers to questions such as these: how will the contracts interact with each other, how much gas will be consumed, and can that be reduced through optimization techniques?

Token Testing

For token generation contracts, run your entire contract from beginning to end to validate every aspect of the contract. This "end-to-end" testing ensures complete confidence in the launch of your contract.

Soon more and more blockchain Dapp projects will invade the market, and there will be a huge need to build expertise to test such applications. Since the blockchain is a new technology, how well and how comprehensively you can test will play a key role in the success of organizations. Like any other previous booms in the IT industry, early adoption will greatly benefit software firms.

CHAPTER 9

Ethereum Use Cases

"The technical side of Ethereum's efficacy is 100 percent an engineering exercise."

—Vitalik Buterin

In previous chapters, you learned about the Ethereum architecture, Solidity programming, and how to debug and deploy using different local and test setups. So far so good; but is that all enough to make you a master in the Ethereum blockchain? The main challenge that the blockchain market faces today is a lack of knowledge about where this technology can be best applied. Business leaders across verticals are struggling to find use cases that would be a good fit for blockchain implementation, and loads of arguments are taking place in this area. As a blockchain expert, it's your job to dream, innovate, come up with ideas, and advise businesses about where this technology can bring maximum benefits.

Ethereum today is the most widely used blockchain framework on the market, and many applications are running in production using this technology. Though Ethereum is not suitable for all scenarios, in this chapter I discuss some real-life use cases in different business verticals and the big players that have already started working in some. Going through these use cases, you will see how and where Ethereum can be best utilized for business value creation. Use cases are described, and in one scenario some basic sample code is provided so that you can use it as a template and amend it as per your business needs to go to production sooner.

© Debajani Mohanty 2018
D. Mohanty, *Ethereum for Architects and Developers*,
https://doi.org/10.1007/978-1-4842-4075-5_9

203

Initial Coin Offering

An initial coin offering (ICO) is the process through which an organization raises funds from potential investors in the market not through regular fiat currency but a standard established cryptocurrency such as Bitcoin or Ethereum. The organization further creates its own new currency, converts the accumulated cryptowealth into the new currency, and assigns that to the investors. The new currency can then be listed on a cryptocurrency exchange, and its price may rise or fall depending upon the success or failure of the venture.

The concept of conducting an initial coin offering through crowdfunding is nothing new. People have invested in IPOs, which work similarly. Why suddenly is this the hottest topic of discussion worldwide? Perhaps because after Bitcoin, when the cryptocurrency market went through a boom and many investors accumulated enough cryptos, they realized that the currency could not be as easily invested in the market as fiat money. So, ICO was created as a mechanism to invest the currency further in the existing market.

ICO Road Map

Figure 9-1 shows the different phases of an ICO so you can comprehend the complete life cycle.

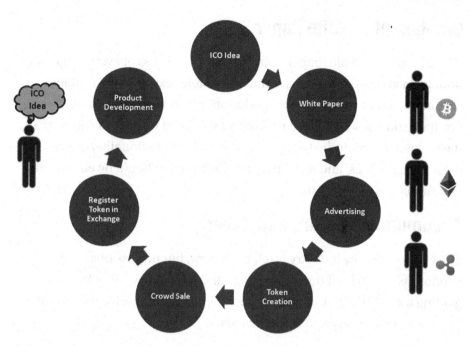

Figure 9-1. *ICO road map*

Idea Conceptualization

The founding member has to come up with an idea that has good potential to attract investment in the market.

Organization Formation and Structuring

Team members have to come together to form the organization. The product that is already conceptualized has to be validated by a market survey and brainstorming.

Announcement of the ICO

The team or the company declares its desire to pursue a project or service by means of an ICO. The interested parties soon start researching the space for further developments.

Creation of a White Paper

A well-explained white paper is crucial for the success of every single ICO project. In about 10 to 15 pages, the white paper explains the problem statement, the business plan as a solution, why it is expected to be a profitable business, the team members associated with the business with their expertise and industry exposure, technical functionality, crowdsale details, legal issues, and timeline. The white paper should be easy to read and simple to understand.

Accumulate Mentors and Experts

The cryptocurrency industry is relatively new, but professionals from various fields can lend their knowledge and experience to ICO teams, guiding them through the process and helping them resolve issues and figure out how to best pursue their goals.

Advertising Campaign

The project development team uses social media, web sites, and threads to promote their ICO. There are several platforms such as Waves, ICONOMI, TokenMarket, and State of Dapps for the sole purpose of promoting and advertising new ICOs. This is done to draw attention to the ICO, maximizing the amount of money that can be gathered.

Token Creation

Finally, the crowdsale event is held, where the new team or organization accepts standard cryptocurrencies such as Bitcoin and ether from investors and assigns them the newly created currency issued by the organization. It's is somewhat similar to an IPO; the difference is that instead of stocks, the organization distributes new currencies or tokens. The price and value of the token are initially set by the company. However, the value will gradually go up or down depending upon the business growth of the new venture.

Listing of New Currency on a Cryptocurrency Exchange

After the crowdsale event is complete, the team tries to get the token listed on as many big cryptocurrency exchanges as possible. Yet some prefer to restrict the ICO to a single exchange. This is the place where contributors to the ICO can then sell, buy more, or exchange their existing new tokens. The market value of the tokens fluctuates as per their demand and supply in the crypto-exchange market. Marketing, press releases and news, and so on, also contribute to the price just like a regular stock in market.

Using the Tokens

The tokens can be used in two ways.

- *Asset-backed security*: All tokens will be given back to the investors who will keep them secure for monetary growth. As the selling organization starts making profits, the value of the tokens will increase accordingly.

- *Utility token*: The investors will instead invest the tokens in the existing business ecosystem. The tokens will be used to buy goods and services in some kind of micro-economy.

Product Development

The project team uses funds that it acquired during the ICO stage in order to push along development, recruit new team members, advertise, and more. The more resources that an ICO gathers, the faster the project development cycle will move along.

The post-ICO phase is all about delivering as much value as possible for customers and token holders. Developing the product and providing clear communication to the public are key parts of that.

Ethereum Request for Comment Standards

Before Ethereum request for comment (ERC) standards, people used to write contracts in Solidity with their own defined functions to impose regulations and transfer cryptocurrencies to different accounts. Soon official protocols such as ERC were introduced for everyone to adhere to.

An ERC represents a bunch of rules for the implementation of a standard API for tokens within smart contracts that are mostly deployed on public Ethereum networks. There are quite a few ERC standards; I will discuss a few in the following sections.

ERC20

ERC20 is a technical standard used for smart contracts on the Ethereum blockchain for implementing tokens. Here, 20 is the number that was assigned to this request. Proposed in 2015, by Fabian Vogelsteller, ERC20 defines a common list of rules and constraints that an Ethereum token has to implement, giving developers a standard pattern to program how new tokens will function within the Ethereum ecosystem. This token protocol has gone viral with crowdfunding companies working on ICO cases. As of January 2018, there were more than 21,000 ERC20 token contracts, with the most successful ERC20 token sales being EOS, Bancor, Qash, and Bankex, raising more than $70 million each.

ERC20 is used as an interface in Solidity with six functions and two events. Developers worldwide have agreed to make an ECR20 token a minimum viable product in market.

You can refer to `https://theethereum.wiki/w/index.php/ERC20_Token_Standard` to learn more.

Functions

The ERC20 interface consists of the following functions. Any contract that implements ERC20 is bound to adhere to these coding standards.

- `totalSupply`: Gets the total token supply in circulation.

- `balanceOf(address _owner) constant returns (uint256 balance)`: Gets the account balance of a specific account with `address _owner`.

- `transfer(address _to, uint256 _value) returns (bool success)`: Allows a specific user to transfer their own tokens of _value amount to address _to.

- `transferFrom(address _from, address _to, uint256 _value) returns (bool success)`: Allows a specific user to transfer _value amount of tokens from address _from to address _to.

- `approve(address _spender, uint256 _value) returns (bool success)`: Allows someone designated as _spender to withdraw from your account, multiple times, up to the _value amount. If this function is called again, it overwrites the current allowance with _value.

- `allowance(address *_owner*, address *_spender*) constant returns (uint256 remaining)`: Allows a limit on which the Ethereum address can manipulate another Ethereum address. Returns the amount that _spender is still allowed to withdraw from _owner.

Events Format

The following events are triggered when relevant actions are executed:

- Transfer(address indexed _from, address indexed _to, uint256 _value): Triggers when tokens are transferred

- Approval(address indexed _owner, address indexed _spender, uint256 _value): Triggers whenever approve(address _spender, uint256 _value) is called

Solution

Let's start creating a digital coin that is a token that you can use to exchange many tangible or intangible units such as loyalty points, IOUs, certificates, and so on.

Let's first create an ERC20.sol interface, as shown in Listing 9-1, that the contract will implement.

Listing 9-1. ERC20.sol Interface

```
pragma solidity ^0.4.0;

interface ERC20 {
    function totalSupply() constant returns
    (uint _totalSupply);
    function balanceOf(address _owner) constant returns
    (uint balance);
    function transfer(address _to, uint _value) returns
    (bool success);
    function transferFrom(address _from, address _to,
    uint _value) returns (bool success);
    function approve(address _spender, uint _value)
    returns (bool success);
```

```
function allowance(address _owner, address _spender)
constant returns (uint remaining);
event Transfer(address indexed _from, address indexed _to,
uint _value);
event Approval(address indexed _owner, address indexed _
spender, uint _value);
}
```

Now let's write the code MyFirstToken.sol that implements the interface, as shown in Listing 9-2.

Listing 9-2. MyFirstToken.sol

```
import "browser/ERC20.sol";

contract MyFirstToken is ERC20 {
    string public constant symbol = "DMY";
    string public constant name = "My First Token";
    uint8 public constant decimals = 18;

    uint private constant __totalSupply = 1000;
    mapping (address => uint) private __balanceOf;
    mapping (address => mapping (address => uint)) private __
    allowances;

    function MyFirstToken() {
            __balanceOf[msg.sender] = __totalSupply;
    }

    function totalSupply() constant returns (uint _totalSupply) {
        _totalSupply = __totalSupply;
    }
```

```
function balanceOf(address _addr) constant returns (uint
balance) {
    return __balanceOf[_addr];
}

function transfer(address _to, uint _value) returns (bool
success) {
    if (_value > 0 && _value <= balanceOf(msg.sender)) {
        __balanceOf[msg.sender] -= _value;
        __balanceOf[_to] += _value;
        return true;
    }
    return false;
}

function transferFrom(address _from, address _to, uint _
value) returns (bool success) {
    if (__allowances[_from][msg.sender] > 0 &&
        _value > 0 &&
        __allowances[_from][msg.sender] >= _value &&
        __balanceOf[_from] >= _value) {
        __balanceOf[_from] -= _value;
        __balanceOf[_to] += _value;
        __allowances[_from][msg.sender] -= _value;
        return true;
    }
    return false;
}

function approve(address _spender, uint _value) returns
(bool success) {
    __allowances[msg.sender][_spender] = _value;
    return true;
}
```

```
function allowance(address _owner, address _spender)
constant returns (uint remaining) {
    return __allowances[_owner][_spender];
}
}
```

The following are a few points to note:

- In the second line, you import the interface, in other words, ERC20.sol.

- Each token has a symbol just as BTC for Bitcoin and ETH for Ethereum. I have named my first coin DMY.

- Most cryptocurrency or tokens come up with a finite supply that you have to mention at the onset of the coin itself. In this case, it's 1,000.

- They also come with decimal places like Bitcoin, the standard being 18.

Deployon Mist

To deploy the contract on Mist and create a new token, follow these steps:

1. Run the Ethereum Wallet on Mist, as shown in Figure 9-2.

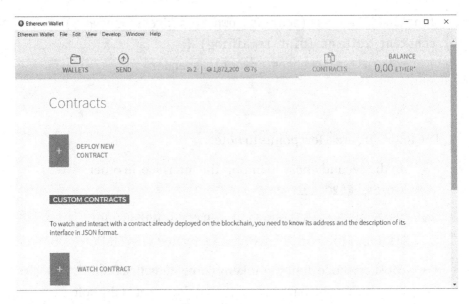

Figure 9-2. Ethereum Wallet on Mist

Open a Mist browser for writing a smart contract.

2. Open the Remix IDE (`https://remix.ethereum.org/`), as shown in Figure 9-3.

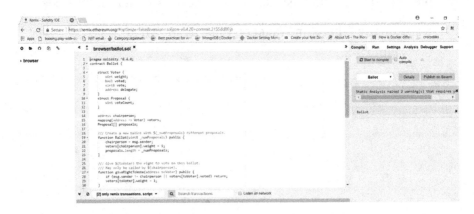

Figure 9-3. Remix browser

3. Search for the ERC20 code that you have just written and paste it into the Remix browser.

4. Compile the code using the Remix IDE and create the token using the Create button.

5. You will be able see the token's address in the IDE. Copy it. Go to the Mist browser and click Watch Token. Paste the contract address from Remix and assign it a name, a symbol, and decimal places. The token is created.

EIP

Ethereum improvement proposals (EIPs) describe standards for smart contracts on the Ethereum platform. You can visit https://github.com/ethereum/EIPs to find many EIPs in draft, accepted, final, and deferred states. You can also create your own EIP as per the guidelines and submit your proposal for acceptance.

Top ERC Tokens That Can Replace ERC20

The ERC20 token standard suffers critical problems, which caused a loss of approximately $3,000,000 in December 2017. The main problem is the lack of an event handling mechanism of the ERC20 standard. The following are the most popular EIPs:

- *ERC223*: Correction of ERC20 errors. ERC223 is a superset of the ERC20 token standard. It is a step toward economic abstraction at the application/contract level allowing the use of tokens as first-class value transfer assets in smart contract development. It is also a safer standard as it doesn't allow token

215

transfers to contracts that don't support token receiving and handling. Go to this web site for more details: `https://github.com/ethereum/EIPs/issues/223`.

- *ERC721*: CryptoKitties and other collections. Find more at `https://github.com/ethereum/EIPs/issues/721`.

- *ERC777*: You can learn more about this token at `https://github.com/ethereum/EIPs/issues/777`.

- *ERC827*: New ERC20; you can learn more at `https://github.com/ethereum/EIPs/issues/827`.

- *ERC948*: Paradise for B2C Businessmen. Read the details at `https://github.com/ethereum/EIPs/issues/948`.

- *ERC884*: White list for investors. Find more at `https://github.com/ethereum/EIPs/pull/884`.

You can find many more at this web site so you know what kind of standards the industry is expecting: `https://eips.ethereum.org/all`.

Use the New Cryptocurrency as a Token

So, you created a new currency in `MyFirstToken.sol` in Listing 9-2. Next let's find out how this new currency can be used as a token or medium of exchange of goods in a new business. I will cover a business scenario where the assembled tokens can be invested in a microfinance project.

Microfinance

As per Investopedia, "Microfinance, also called micro credit, is a type of banking service that is provided to unemployed or low-income individuals or groups who otherwise have no other access to financial services."

The world of mortgages, loans, or any lending platform today is enriched with features such as credit reporting, KYC, and so on, that use the latest technologies such as artificial intelligence and machine learning mostly based on data. However, the clientele of microlending is entirely different. In a country like India where more than 50 percent of the population lives in rural areas, microfinance or micro lending has not been fruitful because the borrower and lenders are completely invisible to each other and borrowers have no proof of a bank account or even proof of address that can be tracked. Most of micro lending happens through local lenders who borrow money from the village bank and then lend it to people who they know in person. However, lenders are bound to keep interest rates high because of the large number of defaulters and the recovery cost.

Solution

Nano peer-to-peer lending via online tracking through Social Security number (or Adhar card ID in India) could bring great benefits to farmers and workers of lower socio-economic segments by including them in financial markets, lowering interest rates, and reducing farmer suicides in countries like India. By keeping the entire ecosystem on a public blockchain, banks could track all the transactions on one big platform. Even insurance companies could follow this information when granting insurance to farmers and other borrowers, which would make recovery easier for lenders.

Let's first explore the stakeholders in this space.

- Investors
- Bank
- Brokers

- Insurance company

- Borrowers

- Vendors

Investors push funds to the entire ecosystem through an ICO, which was discussed earlier in the chapter. Then the bank holds the right of a finite supply of the new currency or token that is created and universally agreed on by all stakeholders as a medium for exchange of goods or services. Now the life cycle goes as follows:

1. The bank identifies the brokers, verifies their documentation in the IPFS store, and assigns them a digital identity.

2. The brokers choose plans provided by the bank with a particular amount, interest rate, and time period; then they sign the contract.

3. The bank assigns tokens to brokers.

4. The broker further identifies potential borrowers, let's say farmers, and upload their verified documents to IPFS.

5. The broker assigns a borrower a digital identity through their ID card (Social Security number or Adhar ID).

6. The broker assigns tokens to the borrower with an interest rate and a time period clause for payback.

7. The broker and borrower also connect to the insurance company to insure the return.

8. The borrower signs the contract and receives the tokens.

9. Part of these tokens go to the insurance company for covering the risk.

10. The borrower goes to the vendors and purchases goods such as tractors, seeds, or fertilizers, and pays in term of tokens.

11. The borrower sells his products on the market and gets profits in real fiat cash (in this case, buyers are not stakeholders).

12. The borrower can buy further tokens from the bank and repay the initially agreed tokens to the broker.

13. The broker returns the tokens to the bank with interest and gets some commission in tokens.

14. The borrower also pays the insurance company in tokens.

15. If the borrower is unable to return the amount, the insurance company pays in tokens to the broker that go to the bank.

In Figure 9-4 you can see the entire ecosystem and the technologies that you can use for this decentralized application. In addition to all this, you can use Whisper for peer-to-peer communication between different parties. Even notifications can be sent using this protocol.

You can use a private blockchain instead of a public blockchain if you want. But in that case the Geth setup as well as the mining part have to be taken care of by the owner. The decision is entirely up to the stakeholders and depends upon the kind of information the contracts deal with.

Refer to Figure 9-4 to understand the entire ecosystem.

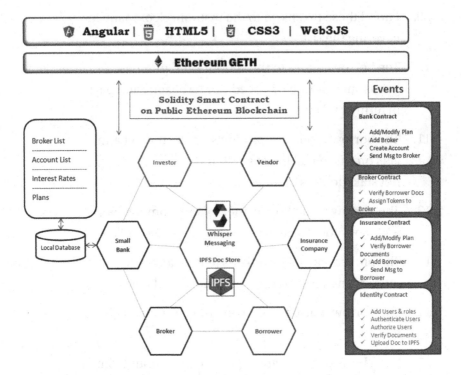

Figure 9-4. System diagram for microfinance Dapp on Ethereum

Now what are the different smart contracts you may have to create? Here are a few of them that come to mind:

- BankPlans.sol: A smart contract for the bank for creating different plans

- BankBroker.sol: A smart contract between the bank and broker

- Deal.sol: A smart contract between the broker, insurance company, and borrower

- Identity.sol: A smart contract for the identity of the all stakeholders

Smart Contract Rules

You can divide these rules into different smart contracts as per business needs.

- The ERC20 token standard will be followed.

- The bank can enforce a number of plans with minimum and maximum amounts that can be lent to borrowers. Also, the minimum and maximum time periods have to be mentioned. Interest rates will be different for different types of loans.

- Lenders, borrowers, insurers, and vendors can be added by the contract creator.

- The lender can initiate the lending process with borrowers by registering them with their Adhar IDs/PAN card number/passport number/Social Security number, and so on, as a source of identity.

- Through the Oraclize service, you will check whether the identity is valid.

- The borrower and insurer have to accept the contract.

- The contract begins. The lender issues the borrower a few tokens.

- The borrower can purchase a few things from vendors using tokens.

However, these contracts and rules are only a few in comparison to all that the business needs, and a variety of business logic would be needed in real projects leading to many more contracts. Also, always follow the best practices in Chapter 6 before creating the contracts so that they are of production strength.

Live Implementation

Here are few examples of how Ethereum has been used by organizations for microfinance:

- Everex utilizes the Ethereum blockchain for all its lending services, allowing clients full transparency into Everex transaction processing with settlement times of less than 30 seconds, low transaction costs, and military-grade security.

- BanQu is a startup seeking to build an economic identity platform on top of the Ethereum blockchain to help people achieve economic sovereignty when traditional financial institutions still won't bank with them.

Real Estate

Fraud is high in land- and property-related transactions. This is often because even if someone claims to be the rightful owner of a piece of land, that person might have been duped by another seller who sold the property with fake documents. Tracking the ownership of a property is crucial in land deals. Let's consider this scenario where a buyer approaches a seller to purchase a piece of land. The buyer asks the seller to show the details of legal ownership of the property. Also, the buyer wants to know the historical data that lists the ownership of the land for the past 100 years.

Solution

Traceability is something justly registered in the Ethereum blockchain storage. The beauty here is data once stored can't be modified or deleted, which gives the blockchain the edge over any traditional database. Let's find out how to trace the previously recorded ownership from the Ethereum blockchain.

You will need two different addresses, one for the buyer and one for the seller. Then you will need a struct for the property details and will need a list of such properties. Listing 9-3 shows details.

Listing 9-3. PropertyTransaction.sol

```solidity
pragma solidity ^0.4.18;

contract PropertyTransaction {
    /**This contract is a basic land registry program where Only
    the contract initiator can assign properties to people may
    be after
    some document verification*/

    Property[] properties; // registered properties
    address landRegistryAdmin; //landRegistryAdmin is the user
    who has initiated the contract

    struct Property{
        uint propertyId; // each property has an unique
        propertyId
        bytes32[] ownershipHistory; //Property ownership is a
        historical data that has a seller, an owner/buyer and a
        date of transaction

    }


    /**PropertySold is an event that informs on success or
    failure of a transaction*/
    event PropertySold(uint propertyId,
                       string ownership,
                       bool flag,
                       string message);
```

```
constructor() public {
    landRegistryAdmin = msg.sender; // initiate the
    landRegistryAdmin as the contract creator and initiate
    some registered properties

    Property memory property0 = Property(0, new bytes32[](0));
    properties.push(property0);
    properties[properties.length-1].ownershipHistory.
    push("Buyer:b0, Seller:s0, DOT:dt0");

    Property memory property1 = Property(1, new bytes32[](0));
    properties.push(property1);
    properties[properties.length-1].ownershipHistory.
    push("Buyer:b1, Seller:s1, DOT:dt1");

    Property memory property2 = Property(2, new bytes32[](0));
    properties.push(property2);
    properties[properties.length-1].ownershipHistory.
    push("Buyer:b2, Seller:s2, DOT:dt2");
}

/**Land registration authority may alter ownership to any
of the existing properties*/
function addNewOwner(uint propertyId, bytes32 ownership)
public {
if (msg.sender != landRegistryAdmin) {
        emit PropertySold(propertyId,
                            bytes32ToString(ownership),
                            false,
                            'Only land registry department
                            can assign ownership to buyer');

    }
```

```
    for (uint i = 0; i < properties.length; i++) {
        if (properties[i].propertyId == propertyId) {
            properties[i].ownershipHistory.push(ownership);
            emit PropertySold(propertyId,
                        bytes32ToString(ownership),
                        true,
                        'New ownership added to existing
                        property');
            break;
        }
    }

    // propertyId does not exist in record, hence create a
    new transaction and add to registered properties
    Property memory property = Property(properties.length,
    new bytes32[](0));
    properties.push(property);
    properties[properties.length-1].ownershipHistory.
    push(ownership);
    emit PropertySold(propertyId,
                        bytes32ToString(ownership),
                        true,
                        'New Property added');
}

function retrievePropertyHistory(uint propertyId) public
view returns(bytes32[]){
    for (uint i = 0; i < properties.length; i++) {
        if (properties[i].propertyId == propertyId) {
            return properties[i].ownershipHistory;
        }
    }
}
```

```
function bytes32ToString(bytes32 x) private pure returns
(string) {
    bytes memory bytesString = new bytes(32);
    uint charCount = 0;
    for (uint j = 0; j < 32; j++) {
        byte char = byte(bytes32(uint(x) * 2 ** (8 * j)));
        if (char != 0) {
            bytesString[charCount] = char;
            charCount++;
        }
    }
    bytes memory bytesStringTrimmed = new bytes(charCount);
    for (j = 0; j < charCount; j++) {
        bytesStringTrimmed[j] = bytesString[j];
    }
    return string(bytesStringTrimmed);
}

}
```

Ethereum Advantages

Land registry is a special type of use case suitable to being implemented on Ethereum. Why?

- Land registration data should be publicly available, traceable, secure, and nonmodifiable.

- Privacy, performance, and scalability are not core features needed in land registry.

Hence, Ethereum is the right kind of public blockchain implementation that will address most land registry requirements.

Live Implementation

Ethereum is largely used for land registry use cases across the world. Let's explore some of the pioneering organizations that have worked in this area so far.

- The Indian state of Andhra Pradesh is a pioneer in blockchain implementations. Partnering with a Swiss product company named ChromaWay (https:// chromaway.com/), it has launched a pilot program for registering their lands to a blockchain-enabled database. The Swiss startup currently made a pilot for the Andhra Pradesh land registry to track the ownership of property.

- Sweden's land-ownership authority, the Lantmäteriet, is soon expected to conduct its first blockchain technology property transaction after two years of testing using ChromaWay.

- Consensys is building a prototype for the government think tank NITI Aayog not only for land registry but also for healthcare, education, supply chain, and more.

- New York–based Synechron is developing a use case for the Dubai government to show how existing deeds for land registry can be handled using the blockchain.

- German startup Slockit wants to enable a peer-to-peer sharing economy where anyone can rent, sell, or share their connected property, be that a car, house, bike, or unused office space without the need to use a middleman.

- After the RERA Act in India Andra Pradesh, Maharastra and many other states in India are considering registration of all their properties in Ethereum-based blockchain storage.

Travel

The delay or even cancellation of flights is not rare nowadays. It can be disastrous to a business and always leads to quite a bit of disappointment. Many travelers are dissuaded to purchase travel insurance just because of the simple fact that often refund procedures are lengthy and not integrated with airline services.

Solution

Let's design an automated insurance compensation Dapp for flight delays. Unlike trains, public buses, and other transport services, flight schedule details are available on the Internet and get updated frequently. There is a huge opportunity for airlines and insurance companies to have a common platform where they can share their public data to make for an easy and smooth insurance business for both of them.

The Dapp will have three types of participants.

- Traveler

- Airline

- Insurance company

The following is the process:

1. The traveler enters the flight details such as date, time, source, and destination.

2. The traveler selects one of the plans and the amount to get insured by and pays for the insurance. This can be done by integrating a payment gateway with a call to the Oraclize service or by using a token.

3. All details are stored on the Ethereum blockchain or optionally on IPFS.

4. At a later date and time, the client again checks the flight schedule.

5. The contract first checks whether the flight date and time are in the future by validating against the data stored in Ethereum or IPFS. It will also check whether the user has not canceled the flight by calling the airline web service through Oraclize. Finally, it will check whether the flight is on time. If the flight gets delayed, then the user will automatically get compensated by the insurance company.

6. A digital identity can also be used to validate the identification of the traveler, and the service can check whether the person is actually traveling on that date and time by connecting to the airline services through Oraclize.

However, there could many other possibilities; for example, the flight might be on time, the user might cancel the flight, or the airline web service might be down for a few minutes. The Solidity contract should be robust enough to handle all the scenarios that the business may incur.

Ethereum Advantages

Here are few of the benefits of using the Ethereum public blockchain in the travel domain:

- It cuts costs by getting rid of the middleman in the claim process.

- It saves time and hassle for the end user.

- The entire process is transparent for all parties involved.

Live Implementations

These are some of the companies using the blockchain in travel:

- Winding Tree
- Cool Cousin
- Webjet
- Sandblock
- Accenture
- Travelchain

Car Insurance

Automobile industries mostly deal with auto insurance as well as have deals with service centers. Despite the coordination, customers often have to fill in multiple forms for insurance claims and have to wait for a long time to get the status of the claim such as whether it's been accepted or rejected.

Solution

Consider the following scenario:

1. Imagine a buyer Reeta visits an automobile dealer to purchase her new car. She selects her dream model, and the dealer offers her an amazing deal on the new model. Also, as part of the purchase process, she's offered an insurance contract, which she agrees to and signs up for, so she provides her personal data along with a start date and end date for the contract. When all the paperwork is

complete, Reeta is given the web site details to a decentralized application with credentials so she can log in at any time if she needs to file a claim. At this point, the contract is written to a block on the blockchain to maintain the transaction.

2. However, in a few months' time, as luck would have it, the car is stolen when she is on a road trip to a nearby town. She reports the incident to the police station nearby and visits the provided web site, logs in, describes the theft, and files her claim with the insurance company. The claim is first processed by the police, who can either confirm or deny the theft. Let's say in this case, the theft is confirmed, and the police attaches a file with a reference number that is written to the IPFS.

3. Once the insurance company monitors all active claims on the blockchain approved by the police station, it submits a reimbursement for the claim. Just as with the previous transactions, the reimbursement is written to the blockchain. The reimbursement can be in terms of money, or it might be tied to a list of repair shops if it was damage instead of a theft.

4. Reeta is a happy customer as she did not have to go through the painful procedure of filling out multiple physical forms or e-forms with all the same data she already provided.

Note that insurance companies have the option to activate or deactivate certain contracts. This doesn't mean contracts that have already been signed by customers will no longer be valid; it simply doesn't allow new signings for these types of contracts. In addition, the insurance company can create new contract templates with different terms and conditions or a different pricing structure.

The app will have four participants, or peers.

- Automobile dealer

- Insurance company

- Police station

- Repair shop

The automobile dealer peer sells the products to a consumer. The insurance peer is the company that provides the insurance for the product (in this example, the car) and that is responsible for processing the claims. The police peer is responsible for verifying the accident or theft claims. The repair shop peer is responsible for repairing the product.

Ethereum Advantages

Insurance claims and realization often involve verification and data exchange between multiple parties. Hence, the blockchain offers a huge opportunity here with the chance to innovate around the way data is exchanged, claims are processed, and fraud is prevented. The blockchain can bring together developers from tech companies, regulators, and insurance companies to create a valuable new insurance management asset.

These are the benefits to customers:

- Superior control

- Reduction on intermediary and trustless exchange

- Transparency and immutability

- Reduction of cost

These are the benefits to the insurer:

- Better efficiency

- Enhanced quality of service delivery while improving confidentiality and integrity of data

- Reduction in fraud

Live Implementations

Here are a few interesting Ethereum-based Dapps used in the insurance domain:

- Etherisc has built many insurance products such as flight delay insurance, hurricane protection, crop insurance, collateral protection for crypto-backed loans, and more on the Ethereum network.

- The French insurance company AXA is using Ethereum's blockchain for a new flight insurance product.

- Dynamis is an Ethereum-based distributed application for P2P insurance.

Legal

In development countries such as India, any legal case takes years to get resolved, and the related parties spend half their lives in different courts just to resolve a single court case.

Solution

Let's consider the following scenario.

Party A and Party B have some legal dispute that first they register in a police station. The matter goes to the lower court where after listening to all the witnesses and reports by the police station, the verdict goes in favor of Party B. However, Party A is not satisfied, so they go to district court where all the previous processes get reiterated. After the verdict of the district court, the parties may prefer to go to the Supreme Court, or highest court of the country. This entire process could take years, and sometimes even some of the witnesses die or travel outside country and hence are unable to appear in court for their side of the story.

A Dapp can be created where each party can add their reports and witnesses. Data can be stored in IPFS, and hashes can be saved in the Ethereum blockchain network. This immutable data can be retrieved again and again as per the needs of different authorities and courts to reanalyze instead of going through the same process again and again.

The app will have the following participants, or peers:

- Party A
- Party B
- Police station
- Witnesses
- Lower court
- Middle court
- Highest court

Ethereum Advantages

If law firms can adopt a common Dapp for sharing data, the same processes need not be reiterated again and again in different courts, and also the verdicts can be stored safely in blockchain storage. This will save time, energy, and money for all parties and can benefit the whole judiciary system.

Education

Fraud in educational and experience certifications has cost the industry millions as organizations have to spend money doing background verification to validate those certificates through neutral third-party companies. The same process of background verification is reiterated every time the candidate switches companies.

Solution

Build an ecosystem for creating, sharing, and verifying blockchain-based educational as well as work certificates. For this, the following is the process:

1. First assign digital certificates to each of the students or employees on the Ethereum blockchain.

2. The student or the employee adds a certificate to the Dapp and applies for approval by the authority, in other words, the university or organization.

3. The authority verifies the student's or employee's records and approves or rejects the certificate.

4. The student/employee approaches another organization where they need to produce the certificate.

5. The student/employee can assign access to the certificate, which has already been verified.

6. The entire data can be stored on the IPFS store, and the hash can be saved on the Ethereum network.

Ethereum Advantages

The following are a few advantages of using a public blockchain network such as Ethereum for background verification:

- There's no need to spend a fortune on background verification through third parties.

- There is no time delay for background verification as all the data is already available online and can save you a lot of time.

- Digital certificates are registered on the Ethereum blockchain and cryptographically signed, so they are tamper-proof.

Live Implementations

Some of the Ethereum-based background verification and related Dapps that are widely used across the world are as follows:

- Edgecoin is in the process of building a Dapp platform for cost-lowering, time-saving, and fraud-protected smart solutions. According to Edgecoin, the technology will revolutionize the education industry as a whole, bringing disruption of the dusty and outdated education system and its certification and approval process.

- Another startup, lynked.world, is also working on verifying education and work-related certificates through verified digital identity.

Healthcare

There are many different electronic medical records systems used in the healthcare industry, each with its own pattern for representing and sharing data. Such a large amount of crucial information is often scattered across multiple facilities, and sometimes it isn't accessible when it is needed, costing money and sometimes even lives.

The portability of medical images is a huge issue as they often fail when transferred. Everyone has been a patient at one time or another, and many of us have had scans (MRIs or CT scans). However, where are those images stored today? CDs containing medical images are often lost. Even when patients do have their CDs, the image files frequently do not work. Also, often there is a need to transfer the existing images and all records of the patient from one hospital to another. How can you securely pass on the data with the permission of the patient without the need of generating it again and without the risk of losing the data? Let's find out.

Solution

Consider the following scenario that discusses how hospitals can securely share patient data through a public blockchain network such as Ethereum:

1. Shelly is expecting her baby in a few months. She visits her gynecologist in Hospital A, who advises her to perform an ultrasonography at regular intervals.

2. Shelly registers to the Ethereum-based blockchain Dapp where she is assigned a unique digital identity.

3. Every time she undergoes an ultrasonography, her images are uploaded to IPFS, and a hash is stored on the Ethereum blockchain against her unique ID.

237

4. Also, blood and other related reports are collected from a lab and uploaded to the Dapp stored against her ID.

5. Unfortunately, in the seventh month, the gynecologist finds a serious issue with the growth of the fetus and advises a cesarean section in another hospital (let's call it Hospital B) with a certain specialty.

6. Now Hospital A and Hospital B are dealing with each other, and they share their information with the approval of the patient. The patient can be directly transferred to Hospital B and may undergo an immediate operation if needed as all the accumulated history of documents can be accessed from the Ethereum network as well as IPFS storage.

Here are the different parties on the Ethereum Dapp:

- The patient
- The lab
- Hospital A
- Hospital B

Ethereum Advantages

You can build a secure, portable, and permanent image solution that leverages the blockchain technology (a permissioned digital ledger).

You can show actual hashes (unique IDs) of several medical images to prove image authenticity.

Using this approach, patients will never lose access to their medical images, and chain of custody will be preserved. All historical data from all different sources can be shared between all parties as and when needed.

The solution offers three core functionalities to enhance medical image portability and immutability, in other words, uploads, storage, and retrieval at superfast speed.

Live Implementations

Here are a few examples of Ethereum-based Dapps that are successfully implemented in the healthcare domain:

- Healthureum is a new revelation in the cryptosphere that combines the blockchain and healthcare to bring the best of both under one roof. The Healthureum platform is designed on an Ethereum-based blockchain using smart contract technology to significantly the improve efficiency and interoperability of healthcare services.

- The London-based blockchain company Medicalchain signed a joint working agreement with the American medical center the Mayo Clinic to use a blockchain for medical record storage.

- Led by the LinkLab and Chronicled, the MediLedger Project kicked off in 2017, successfully bringing competing pharmaceutical manufacturers and wholesalers to the same table. Together, they designed and implemented a process for using the blockchain technology to improve the track-and-trace capabilities for prescription medicine.

Secure Voting and Digital Identity

Voting in its current form in most countries requires the voter to cast their vote from their native state during a scheduled time period, which limits the number of citizens who actually appear on the day of election to fulfil their duties. Also, the entire process takes time and is complex, and it lacks transparency, which has led to electoral fraud, election manipulation, or vote rigging in many countries. Introducing an e-voting system would be a great idea; however, it has many issues to take care of. Issuance of secure digital identity plays a critical role in the success of such a project.

Solution

The solution here is a multilayered process. There are broadly two different solutions you have to cater to.

- Issuance of secure digital identity to individual

- E-voting Dapp

Let's discuss the first part of the system. Creating a digital identity on Ethereum is not an issue because anyone can create an account on the Dapp and use the private key to uniquely identify the person. However, in e-voting, you need to associate the identity with the real person, with the required proof of residency. So, the following is the process of digital identity creation for an e-voting system:

1. An e-voting web application is created on a public Ethereum network that can be accessed on the Internet from a desktop, laptop, or mobile device. The first page of the UI is a login/registration screen.

2. Laura is a lawful citizen of the country for which the Dapp is created. She visits the web site from any device and fills in the registration form. The

form will contain all the required information such as residency proof, passport number, picture, date of birth, place of birth, current address, contact number, and so on, that will be stored on the IPFS, and the IPFS hash will be stored on the Ethereum blockchain with Laura's details.

3. After a few days, Laura will get a call for verification, and her details will be verified by a local government officer through an in-person visit. This is a one-time process.

4. Laura will be issued a digital identity, a public key, and a private key that she can use to log in to the Dapp.

Now let's discuss the e-voting system, a decentralized application where all related stakeholders can exchange data in a hassle-free and transparent way, which will be beneficial for such a complex, time-consuming system. The Dapp will be deployed on a public blockchain network such as Ethereum or be done in private mode depending on the business.

The Dapp will have three types of participants.

- Government agency to check digital certificate

- Election authority

- Voter

Candidates participating in the election will not be participants, though.

The following is the process:

1. The voter already has a digital identification that they can use to cast a vote as a voter ID. Every time the voter logs in, the system will verify the ID for authentication and authorization.

2. The voting process starts on a prescheduled date.

3. The voter casts a vote, and the contract allows it for one time only if the ID and password match. Also, the voting will be valid within the scheduled time period.

4. The voting smart contract will list the votes casted, and the front end will display every vote's ID and the candidate the voter has cast a vote for. No voter name will be displayed.

5. When the voting process is over, the counting process will begin. The process could be a simple one that adds all votes against each, and the one with maximum votes wins. It could also be a weightage-based voting process based on certain logic that the smart contract would evaluate.

6. The result is broadcast to individual screens throughout an event.

The e-voting Dapp is transparent enough so that each voter can always check whether their vote is cast properly. But for others, it remains a secret.

Ethereum Advantages

Using the Ethereum blockchain in e-voting is an ambitious project. These are the benefits:

- Enabling a higher percentage of citizens to cast their votes from any place around the world through a hassle-free voting process.

- It creates a faster and hassle-free process.

- It provides transparency between parties. All stakeholders can watch real-time data and can validate accordingly.

- It eliminates voter fraud.

- The same digital identity can be reused many times for integration with many different applications such as KYC, banking, mortgages, credit reporting, and so on.

Live Implementations

Here are a few examples of how Ethereum is successfully implemented in e-voting. I am sure more such live implementations will follow soon.

- Switzerland's Zug has already taken the first step to digitalize its e-voting through an Ethereum-based Dapp. They are using uPort, a market-leading digital identity solution implemented on an Ethereum Dapp.

- BlockOne ID is another such Dapp based on Ethereum that uses OAuth 2.0 to secure web applications including Facebook, Twitter, and Google.

CHAPTER 10

Ethereum: What Lies Ahead

"I generally support just about every secession attempt that comes along. If in the future there is that kind of a dispute in Ethereum, I'd definitely be quite happy to see Ethereum A go in one direction and Ethereum B go the other."

—Vitalik Buterin

In the past decade, many blockchain and DLT frameworks have flooded the market, but Ethereum is still the favorite of most blockchain lovers. As per a recent report, "Ethereum currently has the most active developer community in the space and has 30 times more developers than the second most active community." The Ethereum blockchain does have some issues, yet it's the market leader in its space, and no other framework is anywhere even close to this framework.

One of the major reasons is because Ethereum has consistently tried to get rid of its loopholes and reinvent itself through new features and versions. Let's discuss them.

The Evolution of Ethereum

Here are some of the major releases of Ethereum and their features.

© Debajani Mohanty 2018
D. Mohanty, *Ethereum for Architects and Developers*,
https://doi.org/10.1007/978-1-4842-4075-5_10

Olympic, May 2015

Also known as version 0.9, Olympic was the first release of Ethereum on the testnet; however, it is now deprecated.

Frontier, July 2015

The official 1.0 release of Ethereum was launched as a public main network. It allowed developers to experiment, mine ether, and begin building Dapps and tools.

Homestead, March 2016

Launched on Pi Day, Homestead was the first production release of Ethereum. It brought many protocol improvements that laid the foundation for future upgrades and for speeding up transactions.

Byzantium Metropolis Phase I, October 2017

This is where we currently are on the Byzantium phase of Ethereum's road map; it's the first part of the Metropolis stage that aims to introduce various privacy and functionality improvements.

Constantinople Metropolis Phase II, Slated for 2018

The main features of this second phase of the Metropolis release will be to smooth out all the issues that may come up in Byzantium and, more importantly, to introduce the proof-of-stake and proof-of-work hybrid chain.

Serenity, Slated for 2018

With this release, Ethereum will completely move from consensus through proof-of-work and proof-of-stake by using a new proof-of-stake model called Casper introduced in Metropolis Constantinople; however, in this release, it will be completely functional.

Scaling of Ethereum

In May 2018, the transaction throughput in Ethereum public blockchain mainnet reached 1 million transactions per day. With the ICO craze taking the market by storm, there is a huge load on the Ethereum network. The scalability of the Ethereum network has been a major concern for its key stakeholders; it needs to support higher future demands if its usage keeps increasing exponentially the way it has been in the past couple of years. Increasing gas costs are also a factor that needs attention.

The major projects that have come forward to solve the scaling and cost issues are the following:

- Casper proof of stake
- Sharding
- Raiden network
- Plasma
- Internet of blockchains

Casper Proof of Stake

Casper is Ethereum's upcoming proof-of-stake (PoS) consensus protocol that I have already discussed. With Casper, the gas fees are expected to go down dramatically, which is a relief for transaction initiators.

Sharding

In Chapter 2, I mentioned how each node on the Ethereum network stores all the states, contract codes, account balances, and so on, and processes the transactions. Currently, this all happens across the network without any parallel processing, which is a killer for scalability and throughput. This issue has raised the following question for the core Ethereum development teams: how we can run this entire ecosystem in a parallel multitasking mode?

Figure 10-1 showcases the working model of sharding. Sharding is a new concept where instead of all nodes verifying the transactions, only a few of them take ownership of mining a portion of the transactions. With this divide-and-conquer logic, the scalability and number of transactions could increase manifolds, attracting more and more big players to embrace Ethereum to replace their existing centralized businesses.

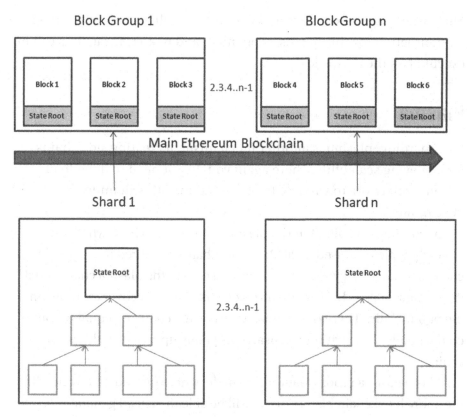

Figure 10-1. Sharding in Ethereum

With sharding, new shard chains will be added to the main Ethereum blockchain network. Hence, there will be no need for miners to download and compute every transaction in the history of the blockchain to validate a new transaction.

Raiden Network

Similar to Bitcoin's Lightening Network, two parties on the blockchain can create side channels and transact with each other's posts, and the transaction is recorded in the main Ethereum blockchain network.

The parties pay some tokens to the network for their mutually agreed on transaction. By this means, even micro and nano transactions can be executed on the network.

Plasma

Like sharding, plasma is another mechanism of creating side chains for achieving scalability where again you do not need to download the entire network to validate the transactions. It's still under development.

According to Vitalik Buterin, plasma allows you to have what the Bitcoin people promised in 2013: private chains anchored into a public chain. specifically, if you have one plasma coin in the plasma chain and if the plasma chain is hacked, then you can use that to recover one coin on the public chain. Therefore, coins on the plasma chain are equal to coins on the public chain without transactions taking up space on the public chain.

Plasma uses a proof-of-authority model where instead of downloading the entire blockchain history, users will be able to instead generate "plasma coins" by sending a deposit to the contract. This ideally will solve both the scalability and gas cost issues.

Internet of Blockchains: Polkadot, Cosmos, Coco

Because the blockchain is already entering the mainstream, there is a huge demand for different blockchain frameworks to be capable of interacting with each other without hindrances. Polkadot, Cosmos, and Coco are projects working in this area, and they will likely hit production in 2018 or 2019, opening the doors to a golden age of data communication in a decentralized way.

Governance

Vitalik Buterin, who cofounded the Ethereum framework, is still actively involved in its development. However, like most open source software applications, Ethereum is also governed by a group of stakeholders.

- Developers like us who develop Dapps with Ethereum

- Users who run Dapps and execute transactions on them

- Miners who validate those transactions

Figure 10-2 shows how any change to the Ethereum framework is introduced and finally implemented.

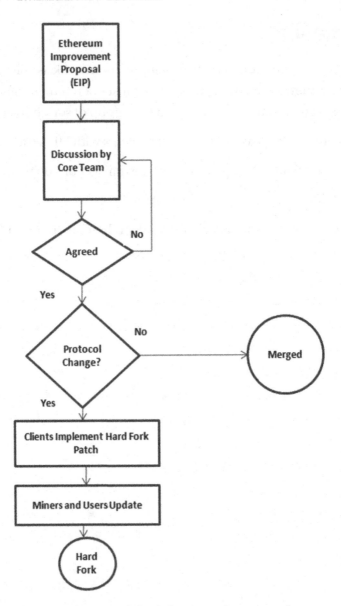

Figure 10-2. *Governance of the Ethereum framework*

Any changes to the existing framework may be raised by anyone as an Ethereum improvement proposal (EIP). Figure 10-2 demonstrates the journey of proposals until they reach the implementation stage.

Many of the EIPs I have already discussed in previous chapters are waiting for approval or the final state. The core Ethereum development team, along with many stakeholders, organizes regular discussions to figure out the future development of the framework.

Conclusion

The blockchain is here to stay and in coming days will entirely transform the communication between organizations and accelerate the way information is exchanged. In the past decade, even as many blockchain frameworks are flooding the market, Ethereum has retained its top position, and worldwide Ethereum lovers are trying their best to upgrade its features to be capable of competing with other mainstream technologies.

The live use cases in this book are in various elementary states. However, now that you know about the entire ecosystem of Ethereum, you can add more complex business logic as per the requirements of your project and take your Ethereum journey to the next level.

References

- "What is RERA and how will it impact the real estate industry and home buyers?": `https://housing.com/news/rera-will-impact-real-estate-industry/`

- "Where do decentralized applications store their data?": `https://safenetforum.org/t/where-do-decentralized-applications-store-their-data/13616`

- *Blockchain and Land Registries: Lessons from the Field*: https://www.youtube.com/watch?v=gbP4AhmYoGU

- "Learning Solidity Part 1: Contract Dev with MetaMask": https://karl.tech/learning-solidity-part-1-deploy-a-contract/

- "Building a smart contract using the command line": https://www.ethereum.org/greeter

- learning-solidity: https://github.com/willitscale/learning-solidity

- "10,000 startups Blockchain Hackathon": https://developer.ibm.com/in/2018/05/15/nasscom-BlockChain-hackathon/

- Oraclize documentation: https://docs.oraclize.it

- ethereum-examples/solidity: https://github.com/oraclize/ethereum-examples/tree/master/solidity

- "Using APIs in Your Ethereum Smart Contract with Oraclize": https://medium.com/coinmonks/using-apis-in-your-ethereum-smart-contract-with-oraclize-95656434292e

- "Oracle evolution: from multi signature algorithm to decentralized Oracles and Ducatur": https://www.openpr.com/news/982416/Oracle-evolution-from-multi-signature-algorithm-to-decentralized-Oracles-and-Ducatur.html

- "Interacting with a Smart Contract through Web3.js (Tutorial)": https://coursetro.com/posts/code/99/Interacting-with-a-Smart-Contract-through-Web3.js-(Tutorial)

- "Understanding The Process Of ICO Life Cycle": https://cryptona.co/understanding-process-ico-life-cycle/

- "Top Ethereum Token Protocols Which May Replace ERC20": https://cointelegraph.com/news/top-ethereum-token-protocols-which-may-replace-erc20

- "Testing for Blockchain – Here's What You Need To Know": https://www.thinksys.com/qa-testing/testing-BlockChain/

- "Ethereum's DAO Wars Soft Fork is a Potential DoS Vector": http://hackingdistributed.com/2016/06/28/ethereum-soft-fork-dos-vector/

- "A History of Bitcoin Hard Forks": https://www.investopedia.com/tech/history-Bitcoin-hard-forks/

- "What is Ethereum Classic? Ethereum vs Ethereum Classic": https://blockgeeks.com/guides/what-is-ethereum-classic/

- "IPFS vs Swarm?": https://www.reddit.com/r/ethereum/comments/3hbqbv/ipfs_vs_swarm/

- "What is the difference between Swarm and IPFS?": https://ethereum.stackexchange.com/questions/2138/what-is-the-difference-between-swarm-and-ipfs

- "IPFS & SWARM": https://github.com/ethersphere/go-ethereum/wiki/IPFS-&-SWARM

- "Blockchains & Distributed Ledger Technologies": https://BlockChainhub.net/BlockChains-and-distributed-ledger-technologies-in-general/

- "Learn to securely share files on the blockchain with IPFS!": https://medium.com/@mycoralhealth/learn-to-securely-share-files-on-the-BlockChain-with-ipfs-219ee47df54c

- "Ethereum Roadmap: Explained": https://thecryptograph.net/ethereum-roadmap-explained/

- *Decentralized Chat*: https://youtu.be/vVsIHCTGjsE

- "How governance works for the Ethereum blockchain": https://dickolsson.com/how-governance-works-for-the-ethereum-blockchain/

- "Scaling Ethereum": https://blockchainhub.net/blog/blog/scaling-ethereum-2/

- "Off-Chain Data Storage: Ethereum & IPFS": https://medium.com/@didil/off-chain-data-storage-ethereum-ipfs-570e030432cf

- "The ultimate end-to-end tutorial to create and deploy a fully decentralized Dapp in Ethereum": https://medium.com/@merunasgrincalaitis/the-ultimate-end-to-end-tutorial-to-create-and-deploy-a-fully-descentralized-dapp-in-ethereum-18f0cf6d7e0e

- "Introduction to IPFS": https://github.com/INFURA/tutorials/wiki/Introduction-to-IPFS

- "Uploading an Image to IPFS": https://medium.com/@angellopozo/uploading-an-image-to-ipfs-e1f65f039da4

- "Microfinance loans recovery on the blockchain—a concept": https://blog.wandx.co/microfinance-loans-recovery-on-the-BlockChain-applications-of-wandx-311355cdd794

- "Microlending Startups Look to Blockchain for Loans": https://www.coindesk.com/microlending-trends-startups-look-BlockChain-loans/

- *India's Blockchain lakshmi Coin prototype | urbanchain Lending Platform*: https://youtu.be/H81eGtivOoE

- "Etherisc Launches Blockchain-powered Flight Delay Insurance For Devcon 3 In Mexico": https://www.the-blockchain.com/2017/10/28/etherisc-launches-blockchain-powered-flight-delay-insurance-devcon-3-mexico/

- "InsurETH runs smart contracts on the Ethereum platform to automate insurance claims and refund in case of flight delays or cancellations": https://fintank.net/2016/06/09/insureth-smart-contracts/

- "Testing time-dependent logic in Ethereum Smart Contracts": https://medium.com/coinmonks/testing-time-dependent-logic-in-ethereum-smart-contracts-1b24845c7f72

- "Testing Time-Based Ethereum Smart Contracts in Solidity Without a Test Suite": https://revelry.co/time-based-ethereum-smart-contracts-solidity/

- "6 Companies Using Blockchain To Change Travel":
  https://www.investopedia.com/news/6-companies-
  using-BlockChain-change-travel-0/

- "Blockchain Voting: The End To End Process": https://
  followmyvote.com/blockchain-voting-the-end-to-
  end-process/

- "A secure internet voting system using Ethereum and
  Zero-Knowledge Proof": https://www.reddit.com/r/
  ethereum/comments/662cy9/a_secure_internet_
  voting_system_using_ethereum/

- "What is a uPort identity?": https://medium.com/
  uport/what-is-a-uport-identity-b790b065809c

- "Different Approaches to Ethereum Identity
  Standards": https://medium.com/uport/different-
  approaches-to-ethereum-identity-standards-
  a09488347c87

- "Zug ID: Exploring the First Publicly Verified
  Blockchain Identity": https://medium.com/uport/
  zug-id-exploring-the-first-publicly-verified-
  blockchain-identity-38bd0ee3702

- "Writing Solidity Unit Tests for Testing Assert(),
  Require() and Revert() Conditions Using Truffle":
  https://medium.com/@kscarbrough1/writing-
  solidity-unit-tests-for-testing-assert-require-
  and-revert-conditions-using-truffle-2e182d91a40f

- Dubai Land Registry: http://www.hackathon.io/
  dubai-land1

Index

A

Application binary interface
    (ABI), 59–62, 102
Artificial intelligence, 197, 217

B

Ballot() function, 96
Bitcoin, 2
BitTorrent protocol, 45
Blockchains
    barrier, 4
    benefits, 13
    block header, 15–16
    Cardano, 33
    consensus (*see* Consensus)
    defined, 2
    DLT (*see* Distributed ledger
        technology (DLT))
    double spending, 18–19
    EOS, 34
    Ethereum forks, 27–28
    features, 5
    fully centralized
        model, 7–9

fully distributed model, 6–7
hard forks, 27
hashing, 19–20
Hedera hashgraph, 34
Hyperledger Fabric, 32
invention, 3
IOTA, 34
Merkle tree, 16–18
MultiChain, 33
OpenChain, 33
public and private
    key, 20–21
Quorum, 32
R3 Corda, 33
Ripple, 32
signatures, 4
smart contracts, 3
soft forks, 26
Symbiont, 33
transactions and
    blocks, 14–15
visibilities
    consortium, 29–30
    private, 29
    public, 29
Business leaders, 203

© Debajani Mohanty 2018
D. Mohanty, *Ethereum for Architects and Developers*,
https://doi.org/10.1007/978-1-4842-4075-5

J, K, L

M, N

Printed in the United States
By Bookmasters